Haunted Ontario 2

Haunted Ontario 2

Best Wishes
Terry B

Terry Boyle

❦

Polar Bear Press
Toronto

Dedicated to Ron Mossop, an elder and a man of great spirit

HAUNTED ONTARIO 2 © 1999 by Terry Boyle. All rights reserved. No part of this book may be used or reproduced in any manner whatsoever without prior written permission except in the case of brief quotations embodied in reviews. For information, contact Polar Bear Press, 35 Prince Andrew Place, Toronto, Ontario M3C 2H2

First edition

distributed by
North 49 Books
35 Prince Andrew Place
Toronto, Ontario M3C 2H2
416 449-4000

Canadian Cataloguing in Publication Data

Boyle, Terry
   Haunted Ontario

First edition
Includes index
ISBN 1-896757-13-8 (v.2)

1. Haunted places – Ontario.   2. Haunted hotels — Ontario   I. Title

BF1472.C3B69 1998   133.1'09713   c98-9318958

Printed in Canada

Table of Contents

Introduction 9

    Ojibway Hotel, Pointe au Baril 11
    University of Toronto, Toronto 21
    Joseph Brant Museum, Burlington 29
    Avon Theatre, Stratford 43
    Calhoun Lodge, Massassauga Provincial Park . . .49
    MacKechnie House, Cobourg 59
    Cherry Hill Restaurant, Mississauga 71
    Time Travellers 83
    Legg's General Store, Birr 97
    Mylar & Loreta's, Singhampton 105
    Carleton Gaol (now the Ottawa Youth Hostel) . .113
    The ghost of Tom Thomson, Canoe Lake 129
    The Orchards, Prince Albert 151

Acknowledgements 161
If you would like to visit 163
Bibliography 165
Index 167
Photo credits 171

Introduction

Despite the books I have written, people still ask me, "Do you believe in ghosts?" I sure do! How could I not believe! I have interviewed so many people who have seen, felt or heard a spirit presence. One has only to listen to them and look into their eyes to know just how real their personal experience was to them. After all, how does anyone explain a push from behind by an unseen force or a bed that levitates three feet off the floor? What about seeing a shadow skirt by out of the corner of your eye or a ghostly figure appear out of thin air and then vanish? How does one explain an object floating through the air on its own and then dropping to the floor at your feet? (That happened to me and I wrote about it in HAUNTED ONTARIO.)

Spirits exist in many different 'forms'. They live in the fourth dimension. These spirits are aware of an existence and place of residence, but they no longer have a concept of time. They live a shadow-existence.

I trust my readers can see that my personal experiences have made me sensitive to the tales and trials of others. It is a fact that I can often 'feel out' a ghost story now as they are quite tangible in some unexplainable way. I also trust that my readers from the first HAUNTED ONTARIO will be equally thrilled with this one. Thank you and enjoy!

Terry Boyle
August 1999

The Ojibway Hotel
Pointe au Baril

The hexagonal tower, the extended dining room wing and the long, roofed verandah help to create a luxurious, yet rustic, resort. The Ojibway Hotel was erected on a 42 acre island in the cottage area of Pointe au Baril in 1906. The original building, opened by Hamilton C. Davis of Rochester, New York, in 1907 was a plain, wooden structure. Further additions on either side were added in 1910.

A plaque outside the hotel reads: "At the turn of the century in a sparsely settled wilderness, Hamilton C. Davis built the Ojibway Hotel, opening this magnificent sweep of Georgian Bay to women in long dresses and men in straw hats and spats who rode in long wooden launches and enjoyed the summer pleasures of the day."

The Ojibway Hotel boosted the economy in an otherwise sparsely employed area. Summer staff arrived from Parry Sound and the Shawanaga Native Reserve each summer. Mr. Davis imported students from the University of Rochester. Charles F. Cole worked there in 1922. "I was discovered by Hamilton C. Davis who recruited me from the freshman class to wrestle with luggage as a bellhop, and to play for dances and beguile the ladies with soothing melodies in the hotel living room." The summer staff all resided on the island with the Native families of Shawanaga camped in tents some distance away.

The resort soon attracted the attention of nearby islanders. Mr. Davis catered to their needs with a post office, a grocery store, a hardware store, a repair shop and an ice-house. Area residents and guests could even have their clothes cleaned in the steam laundry directly behind the hotel, a mere hop from the tower, a very special tower.

A woman dressed in white slowly drifts down the third floor of the majestic Ojibway Hotel. Her delicate feet barely touch the knotted pine floor. Her vacant eyes stare down the hall. She is not looking for anything. In fact she found what she sought a long time ago. It was a dream-come-true, a dream that turned into a nightmare. As the sun dipped beneath the waters of Georgian Bay she watched from a chair in the tower. A short brown rope dangled beside her. She resolved to end her torment but she has never left the Ojibway.

Ruth H. McCuaig, an 85-year-old lifelong resident of the Ojibway Hotel recalls the interior of the main building in her book entitled, OUR POINTE AU BARIL. "The interior remains much the same. Rough cedar posts support the ceilings of the two main ground-floor areas, there are large stone fireplaces in each, and one in the office lobby. Unpeeled white birch forms the railings of the stairways to the upper floors. Only the tower rooms, the most expensive, boasted private bathrooms. Bedrooms were sparsely furnished with plain cots, heavy white bedspreads, a dresser and a chair or two. People did not expect to spend much time in their rooms. For reading or writing letters, they could seek solitude in one of the few, open summerhouses or gazebos overlooking the water."

Ruth agreed to talk about the hotel. She very charmingly told me her memories. "The dining-room tables were set in keeping with the Ojibway theme—birchbark placemats, coasters and napkin rings, all with quill motifs and sweetgrass borders. For a brief period some of the waitresses were even dressed in native costume."

Hotel guests spent their days fishing or canoeing in the morning. Swimming was a pleasure and dinner an opportunity to dress. Ruth describes the attire, "Elaborate, fussy clothing was frowned on, but good-looking skirts and blouses, or simple summer dresses, silk stockings and white shoes were the order of the day for women. Summer flannels, or light duck trousers, shirts, ties and jackets or blazers were worn by the men. Bare feet would have been scorned."

Today the upper floors of the hotel structure are closed. The lounge and dining room are still used and a snack bar was installed in the former kitchen area. Cottagers still use the post office, grocery store, gift shop and gas dock.

The island scenery, then, as now, stirs the emotions. Romance is in the air. Warm, moonlit nights and dancing waters mean hearts can connect. On such an evening in the 1920s, a young, attractive American woman, who worked as a chamber maid, discovered love. He was a handsome, smooth-talking fellow.

As the story goes, she went in search of him one night. He was nowhere to be found. He had not arrived for their usual tryst on the far side of the island. She returned to her quarters on the third floor in the east wing. There she succumbed to tears. A dreadful thought persisted. He had shown some interest in a female guest. Could it be?

She had to know. Stealthily she made her way to the tower room and at the door she heard his voice. In she went and there they were—entwined in a passionate embrace. She fled in horror.

At dusk the next day she waited for the tower room to empty. With a chair from the desk she reached to the rafters and tied a rope; with the noose around her neck she faced the setting sun and kicked the chair away. A dramatic end for her and her nightmare.

Here in the Ojibway Hotel she remains, a white, veiled figure. The young summer employees see her so often they have named her 'The White Lady'. The sightings usually occur in the third floor tower room where she took her life and in the east-wing room she once inhabited. Her spirit usually appears at the end of the day.

However, Ruth McCuaig is adamant that no suicide ever occurred at the hotel. "I knew Hamilton Davis and have spent sixty years in the area. At no time was there ever any mention of a woman hanging herself in the tower room."

"I saw her," said John Cameron, office manager of the Ojibway. "A friend and I were in the process of closing up the buildings down by the dock one night. As we were walking up the front steps to the hotel we both glanced up at the tower. There she was, standing in the window, staring out at the water. She appeared to be in her early 30s and about medium height with shoulder length hair. My friend made a hasty retreat and she vanished."

Bert Bruckland, boatbuilder, barber and hardware store manager reviews a customer's bill. This store also catered to the needs of area islanders.

In 1911 American summer residents with their servants gather in front of the Ojibway before embarking on a boat cruise and picnic on a nearby island.

The family clan strike an amusing pose before attending dinner. Suit jackets and dresses highlight the summer fashions of 1922. Men never went fishing out on the bay without wearing a tie.

The hotel offered laundry service to the cottagers. Native women employed by the Ojibway ironed all day in the laundry.

Ojibway Hotel

'The White Lady' peers from the tower window of the Ojibway Hotel captured on videotape by Rick Omahen of New York. He panned the Ojibway with his camcorder while on a boat cruise and, to his surprise, caught her image. Seconds later she disappeared.

The graffiti on the wall in the east wing room where 'The White Lady' has been sighted and looks out the window. Some people believe she once occupied this room during her stay at the Ojibway.

No one seems to know the woman's name. Everyone at the hotel is aware of the hauntings, but has no specific knowledge of the characters involved. A suicide in a popular hotel in the 1920s would have been quickly covered up, unseemly to discuss and bad for business. No one wants to occupy a room where someone has committed suicide. Haunted hotels were not in vogue as they are today.

Three years ago Christian Dempsey was an employee at the Ojibway. He was returning to the hotel at dusk one evening and entered the front of the building to attend to the snack bar. Later, he left the building through the back entrance. Just as he stepped outside he looked up at the back of the hotel and caught sight of the white-veiled woman looking out her old east wing room on the third floor.

Ed Kernaghan worked at the hotel four years ago and it would seem that he believes in the presence of a spirit at the hotel. According to John, Ed has offered to pay $500 to anyone willing to stay overnight in the tower room. No one has taken him up on his offer yet!

In 1995 a terrible storm struck the islands off Pointe au Baril. John recalls losing electrical power to the resort. The entire complex was in darkness. John said, "One staff member went outside to watch the storm and to his amazement a light was on in the tower room!"

John often works late at night in the administration office on the second floor tower room. His dog, who usually accompanies him, doesn't leave his side while they are in the tower room. No one wants to be the last person to leave, either.

Paul Lloyd is head of maintenance and lives there alone from mid-September to the end of November. I was reminded of THE SHINING, Stephen King's novel about a hotel caretaker whose soul is overtaken by a spirit.

Paul opines, "When you live here alone you have to get a handle on things. I don't let my mind get out of control. I have to function. If you hear a noise your imagination can do anything. I have to live here." Paul does not deny the existence of 'The White Lady', but acknowledges the need to avoid contact.

Her presence is strong in the east-wing room and in the tower. Most of the rooms are locked and the hallway furnishings are gone. It feels as though she will appear any moment.

Calay Hall is a young woman who works at the Ojibway. She would never stay alone in the hotel at night. "I've been coming up here since I was a child. I have often heard moaning and cries from the third floor." She knows there is a woman haunting the tower room.

The Ojibway is still an incredible place of beauty. Gone are the long dresses and the straw hats, the fishing guides and the steamers. But a woman remains behind to remind us of the past.

Two years ago Bruce Bishop, owner of Pleasant Cove Fishing Resort in Pointe au Baril, was conducting a boat tour of the islands as he often does. When he arrived at the Ojibway Hotel, he told his guests about the woman who haunts the tower window. One guest on board used his camcorder to pan the entire hotel, even the tower. It never occurred to him to review it then, but later at home, when he did, there she was, standing in the window.

ABOVE: University College as it appeared in 1890 after the disastrous fire of February 14th.

LEFT: The coat of arms of University College.

The University of Toronto Toronto

In the Norman Archway of University College lovers meet in the twilight. In that darkened passageway to Croft Chapter House they share their fiery passion. No notice is taken of the place itself, of the axe-carved doorway. Another time a star-crossed lover wielded his axe at another pair of lovers. He might still be lurking there.

The downtown University of Toronto campus is haunted by more than one lost soul. Among the ghosts who haunt the campus is a sentinel who keeps the light in The Soldier's Memorial Tower. Since the 1930s, when a workman fell to his death from the tower, a light has been reported in one of the windows of the Memorial Room. Glenn Oldford, a student and tour guide, points out, "Security guards working here feel very uncomfortable. One guard heard someone sneeze, but no one was around. An old man has also been seen in the main hall of Hart House." Some people believe the man could be the caretaker, Robert Beard, who spent his lifetime working at the university.

The strangest tale of all, however, emerges from the grisly murder at University College in September of 1858.

It was here in 1857-58 that talented European stone

masons sculpted gargoyles, cloisters, balustrades and buttresses. These Gothic Revival architectural trimmings highlight the mysterious. You might think that at any given moment one of these gargoyles could move. So many eyes are watching from above. A life-force stares hauntingly from each stone creation.

Paul Diabolos, a young Greek, and Ivan Reznikoff, an older, burly Russian, were two of the stonemasons who worked together during the construction of University College. Ivan was deeply in love with a young woman named Susie. Her father, a British upper-class businessman, disapproved of their union. The lovers kept their affair a secret. They planned to marry when the College was complete.

Ivan had forsaken his cherished vodka for many months to save for his married life with Susie. They had accumulated $500 in her bank account. But something was not quite right. Ivan brooded darkly over Susie's lack of commitment. He had witnessed Paul and Susie exchanging "looks". Was there something there? Rage and jealousy began to build inside him.

A close friend of Ivan's urged him to leave Susie and find a good Russian wife. He invited Ivan to meet him at dusk by the bench near the maple tree across from Croft Chapter House.

Ivan met his friend. James Louden describes what happened next in his book entitled STUDIES OF STUDENT LIFE (1928), "We'll hide inside the little corridor close to that gargoyle where you worked today. See that bench that leans against the trunk? T'is vacant now, but watch it closely, and thou shalt see two lovers sit there arm in arm, as the shadows grow more dense beneath the friendly maple tree."

As the moon rose, two figures did appear. Susie and Paul.

University of Toronto

ABOVE: Trinity College as viewed from Queen Street West in 1860.

The face of Ivan Reznikoff on the left and the smiling face of Paul Diabolos, partly hidden by ivy growing on University College.

They were entangled in each other and in a web of deceit. Ivan watched and fumed with rage.

Susie thought she heard something. She and Paul went to investigate, arm and arm, towards the archway. Paul struck a match but Ivan and his friend were in the shadows. Although they hid, Paul had seen Ivan. He decided to play to Ivan's anger.

The next day the two men worked apart. It was only a matter of time. At the end of the work day Ivan waited by the bench. Suddenly he heard a laugh. Spinning about he saw Paul leaning on the parapet of stone, taunting Ivan from the corridor. Paul had a dagger. Ivan grabbed the axe on the bench and charged the archway. Unable to draw his dagger in time, Paul shielded himself from Ivan's attack. Paul narrowly escaped the blow of the axe, which struck the door. The blows rained upon the door and the frame. Paul escaped through the door as the axe struck deep, embedded in the oak.

Paul flew down the hallway and up the stairs, through a swinging door of glass, and then he slipped. Ivan was upon him. Again he narrowly avoided calamity. Up more stairs. James Louden adds, "At the top of this narrow flight of steps there is a sudden turn towards the east and half a dozen steps lead to the upper landing from which the main steps of the tower ascend. At the angle of the western wall, just at the top, Diabolos, with dagger upright in his hand, waits for his foe."

As Ivan approached, Paul leapt out and his dagger found its mark. With a groan, Ivan dropped dead to the floor.

Paul knew what to do. Beyond the tower door lay the

resting place for Ivan; the well beneath the tower steps would be the perfect grave. He would never be found! Paul dragged the body inside and with the aid of a match he peered into the darkness of the well below. He threw Ivan headfirst down the twenty metre (60 feet) well. Paul took the axe from the front door. With Ivan gone, Paul and Susie eloped out west, taking Ivan's savings with them. Ivan would never be heard from again.

Or would he?

Ivan's restless spirit first appeared on the campus in 1866. In 1890 fire struck at University College. Out of the ashes rose the skeletal remains of Ivan Reznikoff. Glenn Olford adds, "A chaplain gave Ivan a proper burial in the courtyard of the building. He was buried under a tree."

Axe-marks are still visible on the door today at the University of Toronto.

Somehow in 1980, Humphrey Milnes, a Professor of German, was photographed displaying a human skull, purportably to be that of Ivan Reznikoff. As recently as 1996, the skull was reported to still be on display in the Principal's Office. When was Ivan's head found?

John Louden wrote about a man named John Smith who saw and communicated with the spirit of Ivan. "John is always hazy on the point and remembers nothing except that the ghost intended to put in an appearance every Hallowe'en, or Valentine's Day, he was not sure which. John Smith also has a very vivid description of Reznikoff pounding the table, until the glasses jumped, when he was questioned, in a moment of inadvertence, about the teaching of Greek in the College." Obviously, Ivan was still touchy about a little Greek!

Allen Aylesworth, a student at the university, later a member of the House of Commons and Senate, encountered Ivan while walking across the campus. He recalled seeing a thick-set figure of a man. In the course of the meeting, Aylesworth, not thinking him to be anything other than human, invited him back to his student quarters. There they sat by a fire as Ivan told him of his love for Susie and of his death at the hand of Paul Diabolos. He also told Allen about the two faces he and Diabolos carved. He said that his gargoyle was a grotesque face and that Diabolos had carved a smiling one. Ivan said that Diabolos had pointed out that the grotesque face was Ivan and the smiling face was Paul. When Ivan asked Diabolos why, he said that he was laughing at him behind his back!

Aylesworth was shaken. Was this stranger before him really a ghost? Ivan promptly disappeared, his wine half-finished.

Years later when Allen investigated the story, he learned that Ivan's body had been recovered from the stairwell in the fire of 1890. Alylesworth also saw the two sculptured faces positioned on the face of the building near the passageway where Ivan first wielded his axe. The door tells its own tale because it is still in place, axe-marks and all!

Over the years there have been many sightings of the spirit of Ivan Reznikoff on the campus grounds or in the building. When Ivan is around the lights go on and off.

When Glenn Oldford and I were touring the campus we eventually entered the passageway where Ivan left the axe-marks on the door. As Glen recounted some of the history, Reznikoff's name was mentioned. The lights went off.

At dusk I took some pictures of the gargoyles and the door. I used a flash because the light had gone off. I had no sooner finished than the light came on. I took new pictures! Obviously, he was letting me know that he was still around!

Beware of Croft Chapter alcove for a lovers' secret rendezvous. You might resemble Paul and Susie; Ivan might be awaiting their return. Perhaps that's why he stays on campus.

The Joseph Brant Museum Burlington

Author's note: A name in this chapter has been changed to respect the privacy of a woman who had a frightful encounter with a spirit.

A mysterious woman appears in the corridor dressed in a white satin, Victorian gown; a veil covers part of her hair. She searches for the door that will lead her to freedom and the person who has the key to that door. Her appearance is captivating but, nevertheless, chilling. Very few people have seen her. One person to whom she spoke has never fully recovered from the experience. The "Lady in White" is waiting . . . .

This strange presence walks the halls and grounds of the Joseph Brant Museum in Burlington, Ontario. Most people sense nothing out of the ordinary here. In fact, neither staff nor director admit to the existence of a spirit there. Is it denial—or disbelief? A museum is, after all, a storehouse of historical artifacts to educate people about the past, to broaden and expand one's sense of identity in time. Just how much of the 'invisible' past can be housed along with it? Just ask the one visitor who has willingly shared an unforgettable, unexplainable encounter that took place 12 years ago in this museum. The experience was so intense that she never returned until this year when she was asked to reveal her story about the Victorian Lady in White. What connection does this have to Joseph Brant's home or to the hotel that once stood on this site?

Our story begins with Joseph Brant (Thayendanega), a Mohawk leader, who, in 1798, was granted 3,450 acres on Burlington Bay by King George III for service to the Crown during the Seven Year War and the American Revolutionary War. Brant built a home on his property just a few hundred yards to the southwest of the present-day museum. His dwelling was a two-storey house built of timber brought from Kingston by water in 1800. He chose a site at the Head of the Lake overlooking the bay and beyond. He and his wife, Catherine, and their family resided here. In 1807 Joseph Brant died in his home at the age of 60.

Brant's son, John, was 13 when his father passed away and he and his younger sister, Elizabeth, continued to live there with their mother. Little is known of their lives over the years that followed. W.L. Stone, biographer of Joseph Brant, believes that Elizabeth and her husband, William Johnson Kerr, were residing in the old mansion in 1837. Apparently, Elizabeth inherited the home when her brother, John, died in 1832.

In 1845 the Kerrs died and four children were left behind. One son, W.J. Simcoe Kerr, followed in his father's footsteps and graduated from Osgoode Hall in 1862 as a lawyer. It was during this time that the Kerrs, for reasons unknown, resided elsewhere and rented the estate and the farm to a Mr. Henry.

On December 17, 1869, Simcoe Kerr moved back to the

homestead and married Kate Hunter a year later. The couple had no children. Simcoe Kerr died on February 18, 1875 and a year later his sister also passed away. It was during this period that the estate was sold and the homestead was incorporated as the Brant House, a luxurious summer resort. The house had a verandah that swept two sides and many gables. The interior, according to Claire Emery and Barbara Ford in their book FROM PATHWAY TO SKYWAY, was turned into a series of individual motel-like apartments and became a popular spot for vacationers. The Halton Atlas of 1877 featured the Brant estate, which at that time sported 20 acres of gardens, croquet lawns, a bowling green, bathing 'machines', ice cream parlours and a dancing hall. The proprietor of the establishment was J. Morris.

A.B. Coleman eventually purchased the property and in 1899 began the promotion of a second hotel structure adjacent to the Brant House. On July 2, 1902, the new hotel, named the Hotel Brant, opened its doors to the public. Erected at a cost of $100,000, the Hotel Brant was described as "a capacious building with accommodation for 250 guests".

The hotel was very modern and popular. It had elevators, electric lights, sanitary plumbing and hot water heating. This new tourist centre, surrounded by lawns and numerous shade trees, was situated on a high bluff overlooking both Lake Ontario and Hamilton Bay. The hotel's dining room was a massive 900 metres (8,000 square feet) and live music played at mealtimes. Hotel rates were from $2.50 a day up. A special feature of the establishment was a roof garden. An early brochure of the hotel advertised golf, tennis, croquet, bowling on the green, bathing, boating, fishing, cycling and driving, also pin bowling, billiards, pool, bagatelle and ping pong. The manager of these many fine amusements was Thomas Hood. The Brant House complex was renamed The Hotel Brant and Annex.

The Hotel Brant was unable to serve alcohol due to its location in the "dry" part of town. Male guests found this situation quite inconvenient. Mr. Coleman was sensitive to the needs of his guests and thereby resolved to purchase a piece of land across the way and open a country club in the 'wet' section of town to satisfy his thirsty patrons. This building was later remodelled and became known as the Brant Inn. It was destroyed by fire in 1925 and then reconstructed. Famous entertainers such as Sophie Tucker, Ella Fitzgerald, Liberace, Lena Horne and Benny Goodman were frequent entertainers at the Brant Inn.

In August of 1917 the Hotel Brant and Annex was expropriated by the Federal Government and remodelled for use as a soldier's hospital for the wounded. The expansive verandahs were boarded up and remodelled to create wards. Many of the other hotel rooms became operating theatres. The hospital staff resided in the Annex. There are no reports to indicate how many soldiers were treated there or died there.

In the 1930s the remaining veterans were transferred to Toronto. A short time later the Hotel and Annex were vandalized and parts of the building destroyed by fire. Eventually the buildings had to be demolished.

It was T.B. McQuesten, Minister of Highways of Ontario, who was instrumental in the erection of Joseph Brant House. McQuesten recalled the original Brant Annex as a little boy when he and his mother were guests at the hotel. He was so impressed with the history of the area that he felt obligated to ensure that a piece of that history be honoured. On May 23, 1942, the Joseph Brant Museum, a replica of Joseph Brant's home, was officially opened. The museum was situated a few hundred yards from the original site. The loading docks of the Joseph Brant Hospital located to the west are said to be the actual site of the Hotel and Annex.

The first report of a haunting of Joseph Brant's home was recorded as early as 1873 in the American Historical Record and was later recounted in the Hamilton Spectator. One visitor shared his experiences within the building during Brant's ownership.

"This venerable structure presents nearly the same appearance as it did . . .when Captain Brant, with a retinue of 30 servants and surrounded by soldiers, cavaliers in powdered wigs and scarlet coats and all the motley assemblage of that picturesque era, held his barbaric court within its walls. The rumor was reported to me in good faith by a neighboring farmer that the Brant House is haunted."

According to a newspaper account written by Michael Bennett in the Hamilton Spectator, "Visiting psychics have said the supernatural 'heart' of the building lies in the small third-floor room."

Mr. Bennett also refers to an article that appeared in the Hamilton Spectator in 1891. "Grisly find on the Brant property. Investigators digging in a mound discovered the skeleton of a large, male native. Two ivory rings still pierced his nose and alongside him in the grave lay a tomahawk, pipe and knife."

The grand Hotel Brant situated on a high bluff overlooking Lake Ontario. Guests enjoyed lawn bowling, billiards and ping pong or dining while listening to live music.

The Hotel Brant and Annex was remodelled in 1917 to serve as a hospital for wounded soldiers.

Joseph Brant Museum

The Brant Inn served as a country club where gents could enjoy an alcoholic beverage.

The famous Brant Inn during the 1930s featured big bands and famous entertainers such as Sophie Tucker, Benny Goodman and Lena Horne. Guests danced the night away overlooking the moonlit waters of Lake Ontario.

Who was the person and why was he buried here? Certainly the disturbance and removal of a body from its sacred burial place is often cause enough to begin a spirit haunting.

Who really haunts the Joseph Brant Museum?

For years the nursing staff of the second and third floors of the Joseph Brant Hospital have witnessed unusual activity in the museum across the way. The nurses have a very clear view. They have reported lights going off and on in the rooms on the second floor and in the attic space on the third floor; some have seen an apparition walk by a second storey window in the middle of the night. Could it be the 'Lady in White'?

In 1987 a group of Burlington Jaycettes met at the Joseph Brant Museum in the evening. Their meeting was to begin at 8:00 p.m. sharp in the room located to the right on the second floor. The upstairs of the museum is comprised of a short corridor at the top of the stairs and a bookcase on the left. Adjacent to the corridor is a large room on the right which faces the hospital and a smaller exhibition room with a glassed-in case on the left. Past this display room is a small hallway leading to an office and a narrow staircase leading to the attic room on the third floor.

Mary (not her real name) arrived on time and took a seat just inside the doorway. A male friend was seated beside her. Sometime between 8:00 p.m. and 9:30 p.m Mary had the unexpected terror of a visitation.

On a warm spring day recently, Mary, accompanied by a friend, nervously approached the Museum. She did not want to enter the building. She felt fear. It must have been her need to tell her story, to be heard and to be believed that gave her the courage that she needed. Mary is a middle-aged woman of slight build. Her eyes express warmth and sadness at the same time. She knows more than most people will ever realize. She is a sensitive, a person who attracts the spirits of the deceased. It is this gift of sight that terrifies her when she senses evil. With trembling hands, she began her story of what happened that night. She has not stepped foot in the building in all these years since her experience.

Mary had been seated facing north, which meant the doorway leading to the corridor was on her right. For some unknown reason her attention was drawn to the doorway.

"I looked out the door and there she was, standing in the hallway, looking right at me. She made eye contact with me. She was wearing a white dress with long sleeves. Her dark brown hair was partially covered by a veil. It almost looked like a wedding dress, but not quite.

"She was just standing there. I heard her plain as plain can be. She was talking to me. I asked a man seated beside me to look. He couldn't see her. "She appeared to be in her mid-twenties, not beautiful, but not unattractive, either. She was very thin.

"She said 'My name is Eliza. I was born in England in 1847. Don't let my appearance fool you because things are not as they seem'. Then she was gone."

Mary was so frightened that she fled the building.

What has kept Eliza there and what "things are not as they seem"?

The museum volunteer co-ordinator at the time, Ann

Urquhart, was determined to get to the bottom of the haunting. She left a tape recorder running after the museum closed for the night in order to catch the spirit on tape. Michael Bennett in his newspaper article explains, "On at least one occasion Ann Urquhart caught sounds she describes as 'the rustling of papers and a cupboard door closing'."

Mary later said, "I figured out what she meant when she said 'things are not as they seem'. I listened to one tape made by Ann that picked up the sound of coins being dropped on the table. Eliza was a 'woman of the night'."

Michael Bennett surmised, "Speculation is that Eliza was banished from the respectable ground floor rooms of the old Hotel Brant but greeted her visitors on the second floor landing where the encounter took place. The attic room where her presence is most felt by those sensitive to such things corresponds to the room where Eliza did her entertaining."

Mary believes the white dress Eliza was wearing was deceiving. She wasn't as pure as the colour white represents. At the time of the sighting the glass display cabinets situated in the room to the right of the corridor housed a collection of Victorian dresses. Mary said, "I could not walk past the cabinets."

Barbara Teatero, the museum director added, "One day while I was working at my desk I looked down the hallway and saw two woman standing in front of the display case with their hands on the glass. I asked them if I could help them. They replied, 'You have friendly ghosts here'.

Perhaps Eliza's white dress is in the museum's extensive

Victorian collection which is now housed on the first floor of the building and is in storage on the third floor. Perhaps Eliza's world has remained. She is still working in the hotel! Mary certainly wouldn't disagree that Eliza lives in the building. Her experience was real and terrifying. But why terrifying?

"She frightened me. It was how she spoke to me." Eliza's tone of voice carried a menacing force that still remains with Mary today.

Mary remained tense and I felt there was more to her story, 'Mary, this isn't the first ghost you have seen, is it?' I asked.

She hung her head and remained silent. Tears formed in her eyes and streamed down her face. Her friend reached for a tissue. She felt safe enough in the moment to reveal herself.

"In 1978, we thought of moving and looked at a house in Burlington. This fairly modern home had been on the market for a long time. For some reason it wouldn't sell. We wondered why but we bought it.

"One day I was in the kitchen preparing lunch when someone touched me. I was the only person in the house.

"We then discovered that the builder of the home had died constructing the home.

"On another occasion I entered the house and there he was, standing in the room. He had reddish-blonde, curly hair and a beard. He was wearing a plaid shirt and jeans as if dressed for work. I had a picture of Jesus Christ hanging on the wall. I glanced over at the picture and caught him doing the same. We looked at each other and then I knew that it was okay. I called him by his name, Kevin.

"My son never saw him, but did hear his footsteps."

"We lived with this spirit for 15 years. When we moved from the house I cried."

Still dabbing her eyes, Mary glanced down. In that moment you knew her stories were true.

Mary could judge the intent of the two separate spirits. Kevin was kind and unobtrusive. Eliza generated quite a different atmosphere.

I felt it was time for me to seek out Eliza in the museum. I travelled from room to room taking photographs of every nook and cranny. I snapped several shots of the display cases hoping to catch an image of Eliza in the glass. Then I wandered up the narrow staircase to the attic. I knew she was there. I pondered the story that the museum director shared of an experience she and her sister had in the attic.

"My sister and I were up on the third floor putting away costumes in boxes. Suddenly one of the boxes flew up and hit my sister on the shoulder."

Yet when asked if she believes in ghosts? She responds with a hesitant, 'No'.

As I walked around the attic I tried to imagine what this building was like as a hotel. What other spirits haunted this place? What haunting was the writer referring to back in 1873? Who was the male spirit one psychic spoke about on the first floor? I shot some pictures without incident. Little did I realize what would happen next!

I walked into the corridor on the second floor where Eliza had been seen. A floor-to-ceiling bookcase was situated to the right of me. I decided to check the book collection for historical information about Brant's house and the hotel. An elderly gentlemen was seated in a chair about one metre (three feet) away, working at a desk. His job was to catalogue the library. Gazing up to the third shelf I spotted a book I had written back in 1979. Thinking that I might take a look at it again I reached up and placed my hand on the book. Suddenly the book flew off the shelf along with three others. Two of the other books landed on the floor, while the book I had written called UNDER THIS ROOF, managed to strike the gentlemen by the desk on the side of the head, and knock his glasses across the hall. What on earth had happened? My attention went immediately to the man, hoping he wasn't hurt. I found his glasses and returned them to him. In his mind, I had caused the accident. I apologized but I knew full well that I had not done the deed. Eliza had shown her hand. There was no way those books could have fallen off the shelf. I had a strong grip on the one book and had not yet pulled on it at all. It happened fast, with great force. I knew she was there and that Mary was right, Eliza is not a kind spirit. I thanked her for making an appearance.

The Joseph Brant Museum is visited by thousands of tourists each year. Most visitors would never know or sense anything out of the norm. They might miss the truly historical exhibit of Joseph Brant's real home and the Hotel Brant that still stands on the property. Obviously, some of the characters from those days live on as if nothing has changed. Occasionally someone like Mary discovers them again.

The Avon Theatre, Stratford

The lights go down; the curtain goes up. A solitary figure stands in the shadows. The silence is all-encompassing.

Do the dead walk among us? Take heed for they thirst for the souls of the living. And you are here with them. Welcome to the haunted Avon Theatre.

A woman sits in her balcony seat. Her gaze is focused on the actors and actresses on stage. For a brief moment her eye catches the gentleman seated next to her. His face is pale and stone cold. She wonders if he is ill. He turns his head, stares blankly and then slowly vanishes before her eyes. She faints.

There is a phantom in the Avon Theatre in Stratford, Ontario. Could it be the eccentric janitor who once lived in the building, or, perhaps, the theatre owner, Ambrose Small, who mysteriously disappeared and was never found? Maybe it is an actor who once graced the stage here. It is a mystery.

The Avon Theatre, a familiar, downtown Stratford landmark, first opened in 1901 as the Theatre Albert, a well-appointed vaudeville house. The Theatre Albert was the city's first privately-owned, legitimate theatre. Prior to 1901, the theatre in the Stratford City Hall was used for such purposes. Fire struck the City Hall in 1897 and burned it to the ground. 25-year-old Albert Brandenburger, an ambitious entrepreneur, had been bringing theatrical troupes to Stratford for several years and then built his own opera house.

Originally the building had a colonial facade with three front entrances and two small stores at each corner. The front was decorated with four terra cotta pilasters, a cornice of galvanized iron and a small balcony over the main entrance.

The Theatre Albert opened with 'A Female Drummer' featuring Nellie O'Neill and Willis P. Sweatman. It soon became a major entertainment centre and a regular location for many touring productions. Eventually it progressed through a series of names and owners. In May, 1910, it was the Griffin Theatre, in 1924, the Majestic Theatre, in 1929 it became a Stratford movie house, and in 1937 it became the Avon Theatre under the ownership of Sarnia Theatre Ltd. Finally the Stratford Festival rented it in 1956 and purchased it in 1963.

The hauntings of the Avon extend as far back as the early 1920s. Superstition in the theatre is rampant but sometimes with good reason. Some actors and actresses feel that a full dress rehearsal allows all mistakes to come out prior to opening night; some hang good luck charms around their mirrors in the dressing room. 'Break a leg' is a common expression often heard in the wings. Invisible forces of bad luck are thereby acknowledged.

The Avon Theatre

The original Theatre Albert went through many names and changes before it became the Avon Theatre.

John is a retired stage hand who worked in the Avon Theatre from 1953 until he retired in 1996. John has seen many people come and go over the years. Theatre is almost a heritage for him. His father, Fred, worked in this theatre as a stage hand and a projectionist from 1926 to 1942 and John's son is currently employed there. These generations of theatre employees have enough stories to fill a book. John knows about a spirit who watches performances from the balcony and one, perhaps the same, who walks endlessly in the building.

It could be one or more spirits. It could be Ambrose Small who owned the theatre in the early 1900s and disappeared during that time. It could be an old janitor who lived in the alcove off stage left. He never left the building. He was an odd man who liked to tip the bottle. He also disappeared and was never seen again. It seems strange that both these people connected to the theatre disappeared and were never found, nor was their mystery solved. Were they murdered? Is there yet another spirit to be found at Avon Theatre?

Ambrose J. Small was a theatrical entrepreneur who was stage-struck most of his life. His dream was to be a producer. Instead, he purchased a series of theatrical houses across Ontario. He did produce one play but it flopped. Mr. Small's flagship was the old Grand Opera House located at the corner of Richmond and King Streets in London, Ontario. Ambrose Small became wealthy and famous; undoubtedly others were envious.

On December 2, 1919, Small made a million-dollar sale. He took the cheque to the bank and then his wife out to lunch to celebrate. He returned to the Globe Theatre in Toronto and worked part of the afternoon. He left, ostensibly to buy a newspaper, and was never seen again.

John remembers a story his mother once told him many years ago. "My mother told me that Ambrose Small had made an enemy of a theatre manager." Did an enraged theatre manager do him in? Was Ambrose Small murdered in this theatre? Certainly someone still enjoys sitting in the balcony with the "ladies", watching plays to their heart's content.

Employees of Avon will admit to feeling a presence. One theatre employee who worked the midnight shift heard noises in the night every night and confessed to feeling watched and constantly on edge.

John also said, "On one occasion I was working in the left

alcove off the stage. I could hear footsteps around me and above me. At the time there were only two or three of us working in the building. I thought my friends were playing a trick on me. I went up to the attic, thinking that this was where the noise was coming from and that my friends would be there. No one was there. The footsteps were very audible. This is a common experience."

Props and tools go missing in this theatre. They are seldom, if ever, found. Perhaps the old janitor is still cleaning up; perhaps there's a play going on simultaneously in another dimension that needs props!

The lights go up. The curtain goes down. The audience goes home, but the figure in the shadow remains.

Calhoun Lodge
Massassauga Provincial Park

As the sun sinks low on the horizon of Blackstone Harbour, surprised paddlers raise their eyebrows when they hear the sweet strains of a country violin.

Sitting by the camp fire in The Massasauga Provincial Park south of Parry Sound, stories are recounted of the haunting of Calhoun Lodge. Some folks refuse to paddle near the lodge. Other campers deliberately approach the lodge at night to catch a glimpse of a ghostly figure or to hear footsteps approaching on the moist moss-covered rocks that surround the dwellings. Does someone walk here still and serenade the sunset?

Calhoun Lodge at Blackstone Harbour near the Moon River once had a caretaker. He was quite a character, Jerome Cascanette. Most evenings he fancied a drink and a puff of tobacco while he played his fiddle. On a still summer eve his high-pitched chords wafted across the water. He had a history. He was more or less a loner, a man who had fought for his country in World War II as a machine gunner, a man who had witnessed the death of many comrades-at-arms. The carnage of war had changed him. He was a different man. The cries of his comrades who had fallen in battle echoed in his ears. He turned his attention to trapping, guiding, boatbuilding and fiddle playing. Jerome lived a solitary existence in a cabin on Conger (Pine) Lake before he went to work at Calhoun Lodge.

During the 1920s, Joseph Calhoun, a successful lawyer from Cleveland, Ohio, discovered the pristine landscape of Blackstone Harbour. It was here he chose to hunt and fish with his American friends in the spring and in the fall. For many years Joseph or 'Judge' Calhoun as he was often dubbed, was content to camp on his excursions. In 1939 he was presented with the opportunity to purchase the 300 acres where he loved to camp. Local residents, including Jerome's father, William Cascanette, and his uncle were hired to build a main lodge on the property. Local materials were used and a long-time friend by the name of George Washington Brown built the stone chimney. A front porch and a side porch were added later, and a kitchen building was connected to the main lodge by two doors. The Judge was an imposing man, strong and broad, standing 2 metres (6' 4"). He had a passion for gardening and several flower beds adorned the property.

The Calhoun's named their estate 'Willebejobe', derived from the names of the family, William, Betty Jo and Betty.

Hospitality was vital to the Judge and his sensitivity and caring attitude involved him with the local people. He often gave away his vegetables and even the odd chicken to someone in need of food. The door of Calhoun Lodge was always open to anyone who was in need of help or who wanted to stop in for a cool glass of lemonade while fishing.

In 1963 the Judge needed a new caretaker for the lodge

and Jerome Cascanette seemed to be the right choice. Jerome was a thin, wiry man of average height. He settled into the caretakers' house. His duties consisted of grounds maintenance and any odd jobs that needed to be done. In the off- season, Jerome lived at the lodge alone, occasionally returning to his cabin to oversee his trap line.

Loneliness sometimes leads to despair. Jerome was in love with a woman from nearby Woods Bay. His passion was, sadly, unrequited. She chose another man to marry and Jerome lost interest in life.

Joseph Calhoun, smoking a pipe, poses for a picture before heading out on a hunt.

A local resident often delivered mail and food to Jerome at Calhoun Lodge during the winter months. On one occasion a large package was delivered. When Jerome opened the parcel the resident was surprised to see that it was a dress. Apparently, Jerome thought he was going to get the woman, not just the dress, from the Simpson Catalogue!

By the spring of 1968, Jerome was in poor emotional and mental health. He could be heard conversing with his war buddies who had never returned home from the front. He was only 55 years old, a forgotten and forsaken man.

On the morning of Saturday, May 25th, 1968, he rose early. From his closet he selected his Sunday suit, removed if from the hanger and laid his clothes out on the bed. From there he walked out the door, down the stairs to the front door and took the short walk to the water's edge. He washed there and then returned to the house where he dressed in his best.

Then he did something totally out of character and very unorthodox; he broke into the Judge's liquor chest and removed a fine bottle of scotch.

Some time later Jerome left the lodge carrying the scotch and entered the maintenance shed, located between the lodge and his residence. The bottle was set down on the work bench and his attention turned to the tractor. He had a plan. He started up the tractor and closed the shed door, probably sipped a little more scotch and then lay down on the bench and shut his eyes for the last time.

Jerome's body was discovered the next day by the Judge who had just arrived for the season. The Judge knew something was wrong when Jerome failed to meet him at the dock; Jerome was always there to greet him! When he entered the lodge, the Judge noticed that the liquor chest had been broken into. Something was very wrong. Not long after the Judge found Jerome in the maintenance shed, dead.

The Parry Sound Star published a brief account in the paper on May 30th, 1968. "Jerome Cascanette, 55, caretaker for many years on the Moon River property, was found dead on May 25th on property owned by Mr. J. Calhoun of Cleveland, Ohio. The property is located on Blackstone Harbour.

Cpl. Campbell and Police Constable Robinson of Parry Sound Ontario Provincial Police investigated the death. Foul play is not suspected."

The Judge sold Calhoun Lodge in 1972. No one in the family was interested in keeping the property. Joseph Calhoun died later that same year. The Taylor family purchased Calhoun Lodge, but sold it in 1974 to the Ministry of Natural Resources. The Ministry bought the land during the land assembly for a provincial park to be tentatively named Blackstone Harbour Massasauga Wildlands Provincial Park. The buildings remained idle until 1990, when park staff began to work in the area. Restoration work and a general clean-up of Calhoun Lodge were the cooperative efforts of Employment and Immigration Canada, the Parry Sound Nature Club and the Ministry of Natural Resources.

In 1993 the Provincial Park opened for business under the name The Massasauga Provincial Park. This park extends along the east shore of Georgian Bay just south of Parry Sound to the mouth of the Moon River. Massasauga measures almost 21 km (13 miles) from north to south, and just over 12 km (7.5 miles) from east to west at its widest point. 12,810 hectares in size, the park provides important water access to Georgian Bay and the 30,000 islands as well as several adjoining inland lakes.

In the summer of 1993, 18-year-old Scott Thomas was employed as the first tour guide and caretaker of Calhoun Lodge. Coincidentally, his nickname was Jerome, but he had never heard the story of Calhoun Lodge. Scott fell in love with the natural beauty of the park. To him his job seemed like a 'calling'. He was meant to work here and, as of this writing, still does.

In late June of that year Scott found himself working at

Calhoun Lodge, scraping paint off the old generator shed. Little did he know what was in store for him that day. "I was the only person on the property at the time. It was late in the day. I was expecting the staff who were out working on the bay to come back for me. Suddenly I heard footsteps on the nearby moss that covered much of the grounds. I could hear the water squishing out of the moss with each footstep. I knew there was someone behind me. I had decided to turn about quickly before my fellow employees could scare me. I turned and my heart went up in my throat. No one was there."

That night Scott and ten other park employees settled in for the night. They were staying in the caretaker's house. Jerome, of course, was the last person to occupy this abode.

"The girls slept downstairs and the fellows upstairs. That night the girls heard the tinkling of glass. The sound was keeping time.

"Later the next day, Chantel, one of the park employees, and I were leaving the main lodge building and walking towards the caretaker's house when I saw something. I saw a figure standing on the screened-in porch. As we approached the building it disappeared into thin air. It looked like a shadow with a head. I could see right through it. It happened so fast. Chantel had been looking down at her feet to watch where she was going and didn't see the shadow. I thought I was going crazy. I still didn't know anything about Jerome."

That night at dinner Scott and the girls shared their experiences of the day. Their boss told the group about Jerome and how he had committed suicide in the maintenance shed. The dinner conversation died then, too. Scott set a goal for himself and the park, to research the history of Calhoun Lodge and Jerome Cascanette.

What Scott had not suspected was Jerome's need to connect with him. One day late in the summer of 1993, Scott and another park employee were working in the maintenance shed. Scott was up in the rafters and Anthony handed him the boards they were to store. The lads worked away with the radio playing in the background.

Scott explains, "We heard the two-way radio go off. Anthony rushed out of the shed which left me alone up in the rafters. I sat down at the back end of the building and waited. Then I heard footsteps, someone was entering the building. From my position I was unable to see who it was. The footsteps seemed to be going to the back of the building. I was nervous as I crawled around and I called out Anthony's name. There was no response. I was getting really anxious. I rolled over on my belly and looked down to the ground floor. No one was there."

Scott jumped down at that point, sure that Anthony was beneath the building playing a joke on him. He rushed outside. Anthony was up at the house, using the walkie talkie. Scott's thoughts went to Jerome. What was he looking for?

Other stories have been related to Scott, stories of eerie hauntings at Calhoun Lodge. "One person told me that while fishing down by Blackstone Bay he could have sworn he heard fiddle music. However, no fiddler was in view by the shores of Calhoun Lodge. Other people have also mentioned hearing fiddle music as they canoed past the lodge."

In 1996 Scott and three other park employees actually

The old log cabin served as shelter prior to the construction of Calhoun Lodge in the 1930s.

Judge Calhoun, still a great outdoorsman in his later years, paddling his canoe to a favourite fishing spot.

heard Jerome speak. "The four of us were staying overnight in Jerome's old bedroom. We were all lying in our beds telling jokes which were followed by a tremendous amount of laughter. When the jokes stopped, silence followed. It was time to sleep. Then we heard someone else laugh! Everyone was shocked and began to accuse one another. They thought I did it." Apparently Jerome enjoys a good joke, too.

In 1997 two park employees, Kevin and Kris, stayed in Jerome's old bedroom in the caretaker's house. As they lay in their bunks, sharing stories of the day, Kevin saw something just outside the open bedroom door, at the top of the stairs. What on earth was it? Kevin described it as a white mass of light in the shape of a man. Sure that this was all a bad dream, Kevin watched as the spirit floated through the doorway and stopped at the foot of his bed. Unable to speak or believe his eyes he rubbed them to clear his vision and then looked again. The figure was still there. Slowly the figure faded. Kevin said the ghost just vanished within itself.

Then Kris spoke up, "Did you see that?"

Kevin and Kris both agreed that the ghostly figure appeared to be a skinny form at the top of the stairs and increased in size as it entered the room. Scott believes that Kevin and Kris saw Jerome; he believes Jerome still resides in that house.

Scott enjoys the romance of the ghost and celebrates it with poetry and song. If you decide to camp at Massasauga Park you could seek him out. Instead of the violin of Jerome drifting over the water it could be Scott singing "The Ballad of Jerome Cascanette".

Mackechnie House, Cobourg

Elizabeth is lonely, a forgotten child. Her friends have left. She is good at hide-and-seek, so good that few people ever see her. She is, in fact, lost to herself; unaware that she is dead. She might seek you out at Mackechnie House, a bed and breakfast establishment in Cobourg, Ontario. If not Elizabeth, you may encounter a piper or an elderly woman who share her world in this glorious 19th century Greek Revival manor.

The story of Mackechnie House begins back in 1837, when a young man by the name of D'Arcy Boulton relocated to Cobourg and joined his uncle's law firm. D'Arcy was involved in the development of Cobourg. In 1843 he persuaded three brothers, Henry, Andrew and Stuart Mackechnie to leave Scotland and settle in Cobourg. Captain Wallace, a second cousin, also came along.

Cobourg had a bustling harbour, significant for shipping and immigration. In 1823 the population was a mere 350 citizens and by 1840 had grown to 3,300.

William Cattermole recorded this description of Cobourg in 1831, "This is a fine and flourishing village, in which many half-pay officers of his Majesty's Army and

Navy are comfortably settled. Cobourg is a handsome and thriving place. It has its stores in abundance, its post office, printing office, with a newspaper, its churches, chapels, wharfs, lawyers, blacksmiths, inns and innkeeper; hatters, shoe makers, and every convenience which a wealthy grain-purchasing, money-making generation could desire."

Cobourg featured 150 dwellings including 20 stores, three taverns, two schools, a post office, an apothecary, three surgeons, a coach and wagon factory, three furniture warehouses, two brickyards and several mills on the outskirts of the village.

Upon his arrival in 1843, Stuart Mackechnie purchased a piece of property to the west of downtown Cobourg. Stuart built a sizable solid brick "temple form" Greek Revival-style home. The front porch and double French doors at the main entrance displayed the Regency influence of architecture. No one imagined that Stuart would soon become mayor of this settlement.

In 1845 the brothers constructed a huge woolen mill on the site of Robert Henry's grist mill. The three brothers, along with Captain Wallace's son, Sinclair, formed a partnership.

They called their business the Ontario Woolen Mills, an enterprise which soon became the largest woolen mill in British North America.

The Mackechnies enjoyed considerable prosperity. By 1856 the mill was producing 800 metres a day and employing 200 people.

The untimely death of Stuart Mackechnie, at age 36 in 1848, left his widow Anna Marie Barbara Poore, the daughter of English baronet Sir Edward Poore, to manage the estate. As for the remaining Mackechnie brothers, fortunes come and go. Despite the efforts of the mill manager to maintain production and profit, the business faltered and the Bank of Montreal foreclosed in 1858. The other Mackechnie brothers moved on to other things.

Anna Marie Poore Mackechnie expanded the Mackechnie Estate to suit her own needs. In the early 1850s she had another wing added to the north side of the house and there she established a sizable library. Today it serves as a library and a dining area.

In 1862 Anna Marie sold the home to Sheriff James Fortune and his wife, Alice. It was during this period of ownership that the estate became known as Mount Fortune. The location dictated the name. The house stood virtually alone on a high piece of land overlooking the town of Cobourg. Lake Ontario was only a short distance to the southeast. The elevation of the land is no longer what it was in the 1860s, but the inhabitants then could indeed look down from the "Mount".

The Fortunes also increased the size of the home. An extensive addition at the back is the kitchen today.

The Sheriff oversaw the operations of the gaol and other community matters but his career ended in 1864, when he died of Brights disease at the early age of 51. Rumour indicated some sort of political scandal and certainly his financial arrangement with his wife was very unusual for the time. The deed to the house and property was only in his wife's name. Obviously, the Sheriff wanted to protect his property from his financial dealings.

In 1866 an infantry battalion associated with the Cobourg Militia was billeted behind the Mackechnie House shortly after the beginning of the Fenian raids in Niagara. The Fenian Brotherhood was a society of Irishmen who sought to force the British to give Ireland its freedom. Many Irish-Americans inhabiting the United States near the Canadian border had banded together to attack British-controlled soil. The fear of Fenian attacks continued for five years. For part of that time the Mackechnie house served as an Officers' Mess in the Cobourg area. A piper was one of the soldiers.

Alice Fortune sold the estate in 1869 and ownership of the home changed several times before Cathryn Thompson and Ian Woodburn bought Mackechnie House in 1993 from Arnold Burgis. They moved in with their son, Rory. By then the house was in a state of disrepair and every room was full of heirlooms and boxes of Burgis possessions. He had been living in this spacious home alone since the recent death of his mother.

Ian specializes in restorations and renovations; Cathryn was a business executive in need of a change. A bed and breakfast and catering enterprise seemed the perfect solution. They had a brochure printed:

"Built for Upper Canada settler Stuart Mackechnie in the grand and glorious Greek Revival style, Mackechnie House is the finest remaining example of this type of monumental domestic architecture in the Cobourg area.

"The Mackechnie House Ghost dates from around the same time (mid-1800s), and local rumour spins tales of a Highland Infantry Company Bagpiper's untimely demise.

Duty-conscious to the end (and beyond, it seems!) the only wailing he indulges in is that of his pipes, and modern encounters with this shy fellow, though delightful, can be sporadic.

"However, a reluctant ghost is no reason to put off your visit to Cobourg. By the time you've seen all there is to see in this history-and event-packed corner of Northumberland County, you'd probably just sleep through his nocturnal perambulations anyway!"

When Cathryn first moved into the home she had no idea it was haunted. In fact, she had never been exposed to any unexplained spirit activity. "I am not extremely sensitive to spirits. I didn't have an experience until I moved here.

"During the first year we experienced something very unusual. One day a friend and her seven-year-old daughter were sitting in the kitchen. We were chatting away when suddenly her daughter pointed toward the library and said, 'Who is the little girl?' We didn't know what she was talking about. We couldn't see anything."

On three separate occasions, psychics who were staying in the house reported the existence of three spirits in the home, an old woman, a little girl named Elizabeth and a bagpipe-playing soldier.

According to one psychic, Elizabeth longs to play with other children. She is seldom seen because she doesn't want to frighten anyone. Elizabeth lives in the attic on the third floor of the house, a prisoner of her own world.

At the top of the stairs on the landing to the right is the Rose Room. This is where Mrs. Burgis is said to have died.

Guests staying overnight in the Rose room report a cold spot near the table and chairs.

Could she be the elderly spirit? When Cathryn first began decorating this room she felt the need to choose wallpaper with roses. She even went a step further and had a dried rose framed to hang in the room. The bedspreads also reflected the rose theme. Cathryn is not attracted to roses. In fact, she had no idea why she felt compelled to decorate in this manner. It was later that she discovered that roses just happened to be Mrs. Burgis' favourite flower.

There is a cold spot in this room a short distance from the bed. Guests often complain about feeling a cold draft in this one area of the room. According to Cathryn there is a reason for this. Near the end of her life Mrs Burgis was quite ill and bedridden. The nurse staying with her said she tried to get out of bed because she thought that someone had come for her. Mrs Burgis rose from her bed and stepped forward to meet a man who only she could see. Then she collapsed and died.

Some people who have stayed in this room have told Cathryn that they could never get warm, even in the summertime. One overnight guest said they felt the spirit tucking them in at night.

Cathryn has to smooth out the blankets on the bed almost every day. It's as if someone lays there on a daily basis. People often complain about the loss of personal items when they stay there. They blame it on forgetfulness or their partner whom they feel certain has placed it somewhere else. Then just when they give up, the item reappears, right where they know they left it.

One day Cathryn was about to place a phone call. She carefully took one earring off and placed it on the table before lifting the receiver to her ear. After a lengthy conversation she put the phone down and reached for her earring. It was gone!

"Many things go missing, such as clothing. I have lost a skirt, a belt and some jewellery. These belongings have not yet returned."

Ian often still spends his weekends restoring areas of the house. The disappearance of tools is also not an uncommon occurrence.

One day their son Rory asked his dad to hook up the video machine. Ian recalls what happened. "I needed a pair of pliers to do the job. I remember placing the pliers back in the tool box after the job was completed. The next day they were gone. I looked everywhere. Three days later I walked by the video machine and there they were right in front of it, in plain view on the floor."

When asked if he believes in ghosts Ian's reply is, "My mother had just died. I was sitting alone in the living room and I could sense a strong presence. I knew I was not alone in the room. That was it."

One morning a guest named Joanne complained over breakfast about not getting much sleep the night before. Cathryn explains, "Joanne told me a little girl and an elderly woman visited her during the night in her room. Joanne had asked them not to show themselves although she could hear them speak. Joanne said the girl, Elizabeth, was 12 years old. At first Elizabeth told her that she had been dramatically murdered in the house. However, she later said she had died of an illness. She said she was waiting to leave. It was Elizabeth and the elderly woman who told her there was another spirit in the house."

That other spirit could be the Scottish bagpiper who apparently was billeted here back in 1866. Cathryn says, "People who have lived around Cobourg for a number of years and as children played in the house can vividly recall hearing his music. A number of people I have met claimed to have seen him." Sarah attended a birthday party in the house back in the late 1960s and this is what she saw:

"There was a group of us playing on the second floor of the home. We had never heard of ghosts before. For whatever reason I looked up at the staircase that leads to the third floor. I caught a glimpse of the back of a man from the waist down just as he was turning the top of the stairs. I saw one leg. He was wearing a black shoe and a kilt. I knew it was a kilt because I was a highland dancer at the time. The kilt was the black watch tartan with dark blue and green and a bit of yellow. I wasn't the only one who saw him. We rushed up the stairs but there was nothing there."

Little is known about this piper or his reason for remaining in the house. Cathryn and Ian, unlike others, have never seen him or heard his music.

In December of 1997 Cathryn did encounter one of the spirits. "Back then I was usually rising about 4 a.m. to begin my catering work. I had one businessman who was a guest staying for the week. He rose for breakfast promptly at 7:15 a.m. I always made sure I had coffee ready before he arrived in the kitchen. This particular morning I slept in. I awakened at 6:30 p.m. to the sound of footsteps going down the stairs. Thinking it was him I rushed down to the kitchen to hit the switch on the coffee percolator. No one was there but someone had helped me out: just as I entered the kitchen the coffee percolator started to drip. I stood there in shock."

On yet another occasion Cathryn was astounded by the generosity of the spirits.

"I always know how much money I have in my wallet. On this particular day I was going out for lunch with some friends. I knew I had two $5.00 bills in my wallet. Before reaching the restaurant I gave one $5.00 bill to my son before dropping him off. I then stopped at a convenience store and spent the other $5.00. During lunch a musical group entertained us. I decided to have the waiter deliver $5.00 and a request to one of the players. I pulled my wallet out and to my amazement discovered the $5.00 was gone. I made a fuss about missing this money. I couldn't believe it. Then I realized on the way home, after picking up my son, that I had spent the money at the variety store. Feeling quite foolish with myself I drove home. There at the top of the basement stairs was a soaking-wet $5.00 bill. I then remembered the psychics saying the spirits were there to help me."

Cathryn and Ian have renovated the north wing at the back of the house into an apartment that they rent out. A previous tenant once borrowed two books from Cathryn. After she had read the books they were returned. Cathryn remembers placing them on her desk. One day she noticed that one book had disappeared. A short time later her tenant discovered the missing book back in her apartment standing upright on the floor.

The same tenant often complained about missing her clip-on sunglasses. Each time she would have to go out and buy another pair. Then one day the missing sunglasses appeared. Three pairs of sunglasses, all clipped together, were discovered on a shelf.

Mackechnie House hosts many celebrations. One evening Cathryn catered for a woman who wanted to celebrate her 50th birthday by holding a seance in the house. She hired a psychic and invited 18 people to attend.

According to Cathryn, "It was a strange experience. They held the seance in the library and dining room. Holding hands they waited and waited. Then someone spoke, 'There is something in the basement'."

Cathryn said, "I believe this. I have seen a pink light or beam travel by me. I can also feel someone standing behind me. At the top of the basement stairs you often get the feeling that someone is walking by." This is the same place where the $5.00 bill mysteriously appeared.

When it comes to spirits one never knows what will happen next. This was true for Cathryn one day last year when she went shopping for antiques in Port Hope.

"I was in Port Hope visiting an antique shop on the main street. The woman who owns the store said to me, 'Have you seen the ghost?'

"I replied, 'No, but we understand we have three ghosts. One of them is a little girl, another an elderly woman and there is a bag piper.

"I then said to the woman, 'I wonder if the elderly woman is Mrs Burgis?'

"Then the lady said to me, 'My dead grandmother is with me.' I said, 'Oh yes, I feel that way about my grandmother, too.'

"The woman was looking at me with tears in her eyes. 'You don't understand. My grandmother is talking to me right now. And Mrs Burgis has asked my grandmother to ask you to give her permission to leave this plane.'

"I was at a loss for words. I said 'All right'.

"I came home and went to the room where Mrs Burgis had died. I then addressed her. I said 'You are more than welcome to stay but if you want to go, please do so.'"

It would seem she didn't go. Just a week after I interviewed the family, a guest staying in the Rose Room was hugged. During the night the guest felt a coldness around her shoulders and neck. If felt as though someone was embracing her. Was it Mrs Burgis?

When did Elizabeth arrive and why did she stay? How did the bagpiper die? Why did Mrs Burgis not leave with the male figure at her bedside? Who or what is the presence in the basement?

Elizabeth and Mrs Burgis seem to have a friendship or at least communication with one another. Is this a common phenomenon in the spirit dimension? Other ghosts at other sites seem oblivious to one another. Does this mean they were connected in life or is this just another coincidence?

At least Elizabeth has someone to talk to! Maybe you should pay her a visit!

Cherry Hill Restaurant Mississauga

It is early 1900. A group of spiritualists are secretly gathered in a private location to share a ritual. They want to connect with their dead relatives or friends. Most participants are impassioned and perhaps even obsessed with exploring this unknown realm. Their imaginations are keen, not necessarily reasoned. They sit around the table, arms outstretched, guided by a Shakespearean actor who instructs them to lightly rest their hands on a heart-shaped object in the centre of a homemade ouija board. One candle flickering on the pine mantlepiece casts eerie shadows about the room.

They begin. 'Spirit, if you are there, give us a sign'. The movable pointer quickly slides to the word 'yes'.

'Do you have a name?' The pointer flies around the alphabet to spell, 'Two Feathers'.

'Why are you here?' A sudden gust of wind in the room causes the candle flame to cast ominous shadows around the room. The candle goes out. Fear- gripped participants flee. Will the spirit remain?

Here we are in 1999, many years and, perhaps, many spirits later. We are at Cherry Hill House.

Built by Joseph Silverthorn, it is the oldest surviving house in Mississauga. Joseph was a United Empire Loyalist who married 15 year- old Jane Chisholm in Queenston Heights in April of 1807 and moved to what is now Mississauga. There he built a 6 metre by 4 metre (18 foot by 14 foot) cabin where they lived in harmony with the Ojibwa who wandered in small groups hunting and fishing. They recorded how the Native peoples often visited by walking into the cabin unannounced to sit and watch them silently. Initially this was alarming to Jane, especially when Joseph was away. By 1815 Joseph had begun construction of a stately home built with his own trees and with fieldstone gathered from a nearby stream, later called Etobicoke Creek. This magnificent structure was completed by 1822.

Joseph and Jane planted a mile of cherry trees from the front gate to the barn, encircling the homestead and inspiring the name 'Cherry Hill' for the estate. These were cherry trees originally brought to New Jersey from an ancestral home in England by Oliver Silverthorn in 1700. Joseph maintained the tradition when he brought young saplings from that home to his new estate.

The Silverthorns had 12 children, nine daughters and three sons. One child died at birth. They were among the first white children to be born in Toronto Township.

On July 12, 1879, Joseph passed away, leaving Jane and three daughters, Augusta, Jane and Helen to manage the estate. Jane died in November of the same year. By 1907 Augusta was the sole owner of Cherry Hill. On December 10th of that year she passed away leaving the estate to her favourite nephew, William Stanislas Romain.

William was an actor, a dramatic artist and a vocalist who trained in England and began his career at age 18. William was considered to be quite an eccentric; he dressed oddly, perhaps due to his profession, which he took seriously. He acted in many countries where he worked alongside talented people such as Sarah Bernhardt and Mary Pickford. William was also drawn to spiritualism.

Kathleen Hicks, author and historian, has spent the last few years compiling a book about the Silverthorn family and Cherry Hill House. Kathleen was important in the movement to save the building from demolition in 1973.

Kathleen writes, "Mr Romain apparently didn't appreciate his inheritance, for it was after he took over the Silverthorn homestead that the house was let go to gradual ruin. William rented parts of the house to several families, while he maintained a section of the house for himself. In the early 1950s a friend of the family, Miss Lindsay, rented the home. William died at the age of 84 in 1951."

Unfortunately, most of his tenants felt that William was responsible for repairs. Kathleen adds, "The house gradually deteriorated, until the front veranda was down, and a gray pallor clung to the unpainted interior." In 1973 the home was threatened with demolition until a group of concerned citizens and a developer moved the house moved from its original location at the corner of Dundas Street and Cawthra, stands a few hundred yards away to 680 Silvercreek Boulevard. The house was completely renovated and restored to its original grandeur by The Triomphe Group. Perhaps it was fitting that the house opened to the public on the eve of Hallowe'en, 1979, as the Cherry Hill House Restaurant.

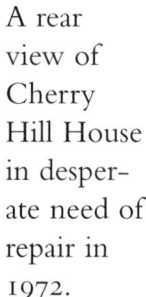

A rear view of Cherry Hill House in desperate need of repair in 1972.

Kathleen writes, "William held elaborate parties in the driving shed and he and his guests would dress as Shakespearean characters." She also writes about his spiritualism and the seances at Cherry Hill House. We can only speculate about the results of such activities.

For years stories have circulated about the hauntings of Cherry Hill House. The appearance of any dilapidated old house will conjure up spooky images in many minds, whispers begin and before you know it, it becomes the gospel truth. However, these hauntings were documented.

The first written account of any haunting at Cherry Hill House appeared in *The Toronto Star* on October 26, 1980, written by Frank Jones and entitled 'Visiting Our Restless Spirits'. In 1973 the first reported sighting occurred according to Mr. Jones. "In that year, a security guard, Ron Land, was sitting outside the deserted house guarding it one night when he saw a white figure rise out of a pile of earth, bran-

The restored Cherry Hill House.

dishing a sword. Land jumped out of his car, and his dog, Cindy, ran towards the figure. The dog shied away, and as the figure came towards him Land, too, turned and fled. Police kept watch the next night but saw nothing."

Could this apparition who rose from the soil be a spirit lingering from a seance half a century ago?

After the house was moved down the street another security guard witnessed the unbelievable. He saw a girl dressed in white sitting on a white horse inside the house.

On another occasion a medium who was dining at the restaurant reported that the girl wearing white was the spirit of a 16 year-old. Her name was Miranda and she burned to death in the house while making candles. According to Kathleen Hicks, there was never a Silverthorn named Miranda, nor any mention of a fire in the house. It may be possible, however, that a girl by this name resided in the house during the years that William had tenants.

Reports of Native apparitions and rumours about Native burial grounds have circulated and been documented by writers including John Robert Columbo. These include accounts of old Native faces floating out of the fireplace, workmen's tools disappearing and bizarre accidents on stairs.

Historian Kathleen Hicks maintains that Cherry Hill was never constructed on top of a Native burial ground. However, some people believe the building's foundation blocks came from a nearby field that was once used as an Indian burial site.

Once again Ms. Hicks helps to clarify this by adding, "The stones used during the construction of the house were transported by Joseph Silverthorn himself from the Etobicoke Creek to the property." Although there is a Native presence in the building, it is, in her estimation, in no way related to a burial ground.

Anita is a young woman who works as a bartender and is the supervisor of the Duke of Marlborugh, an authentic British Pub located on the lower level of Cherry Hill House Restaurant. The pub is quaint, with its flagstone floor and fireplace at the far end. A bar with a few stools is situated to the right of the main entrance and a short corridor leads to the washrooms and to a flight of stairs up to the first floor. Anita had heard stories from friends about hauntings at Cherry Hill before she worked there as an employee. These stories primarily centered around a presence in the attic of the building. Naturally, she had no idea that her first day on the job would reveal some truth about those stories.

Cherry Hill Restaurant

Anita is an experienced waitress, focused on her work and very capable. Nonetheless, on her first day at the job she had an accident. "I was carrying a tray of drinks to a table and fell. Something tripped me. I turned around but nothing was there. I am superstitious and felt I needed to respond in some way. So a week later I went up to the attic and spoke to the spirits. I said, 'Please leave me alone. I like you and mean no harm to you'."

Her next encounter happened when she found someone standing just a few feet away from her. "It was 10:30 p.m. There were two or three customers sitting at the bar. I was in the process of pouring a drink when I caught sight of a figure out of the corner of my eye. Right at the doorway of the storage room and not far from the bar was a Native man. He was tall, about six feet, four inches, and was wearing light-beige deerskin. I could also see his deerskin leggings. He had long, dark-brown hair. He could have been in his 30s. I turned quickly to get a better look at him and he was gone."

On another occasion a husband, wife and mother-in-law arrived for an evening meal. They were seated on the first floor in front of the fireplace. In the middle of a conversation, the older woman suddenly caught a glimpse of a Native woman by the fireplace. She questioned what she was seeing, but no one else could see the woman.

The staff also see an old Native man floating in mid-air or walking down the stairs. One worker felt a hand grip his shoulder. When he turned around he saw the elderly native standing behind him. Then he vanished.

Anita is certain that spirits inhabit Cherry Hill

Restaurant. In fact she has now had several different experiences, especially after closing time. "I often hear footsteps on the first floor situated above the pub. One minute the footsteps are above the bar on the main floor and the next minute you can hear them at the other end of the pub. The footsteps are heard on a regular basis. One night after closing the pub, about 2:00 a.m., I put the radio on to help me get in motion. As I left the bar to wipe the first table, the radio turned off. I walked back and as soon as I turned the corner of the bar the radio came back on. This happened to me four times. I had had enough, closed up and left the building."

On another occasion shortly after closing time Anita and her boyfriend experienced a very disconcerting sound the sound of a hissing cat. They left quickly.

Anna Maria and Guerrino Staropoli purchased Cherry Hill House Restaurant in 1985 from the Triomphe chain. Guerrino related an experience that happened to him when they first took over the business. "I was working late one night in the office located on the second floor when I heard two knocks." Tom thought the knocking was coming from the hallway outside the office door. Then he realized it was actually within the wall that separated the office from another room.

The stairway to the attic is also located in the office area. Tom remembers an incident when friends were seated in the main floor dining area on the right-hand side of the building. The diners were the only ones in the room. Suddenly one of the wall lights near their table began to flash on and off while the other lights in the room remained on.

A previous owner of Cherry Hill House Restaurant reported that when he closed up at night he would make sure all the lights were off before leaving the building. As he was driving away he would often catch sight of a light on in the attic window of the building. He would return to the restaurant, go up the stairs to the attic and turn the light off; the moment he would drive away the light would come on again!

Alicia was a long-term employee of the Cherry Hill House Restaurant, a waitress there from 1985 to 1996. She actually walked right through one of the spirits. "My first experience was when I was waitressing in the pub. It was about 9:00 p.m. when I took a short break and went to the ladies' washroom. As I was leaving the washroom I walked right through what seemed to be a fog. The fog was actually in the shape of a human. It was very tall and large. My body was shaking and felt extremely cold when I walked through it. I returned to the bar and shared my experience with the bartender.

"On another occasion I was serving two girls seated at a table by the fireplace. One girl looked at me and quivered. The other girl said, 'Is there a ghost here?' Her friend was visibly shaken and was feeling cold. Apparently, she was very sensitive and felt the presence of a spirit. They quickly left the pub."

Alicia is certain that the spirits in the house have never harmed anyone; in fact, they are quite pleasant. One evening she was alone in the evening counting the cash. "My back was turned to the seating area in the pub. I felt someone was watching me. I was scared in the beginning, but I got used to it. The same thing happens when you go upstairs to the office late at night. You can feel a presence."

Some incidences are extraordinary phenomena, "The power had gone out and we lit some candles for light in the restaurant. I went outside to see the whole neighborhood in darkness, including the restaurant. As I walked around to the back of the building I looked up and to my amazement a light was on in every window of the attic. Someone was there!" It would seem the spirits have their own source of electricity!

Music is another way in which spirits express themselves. Some spiritualists believe that all thought ultimately expresses itself through sound. This sound is often described as a series of ever-changing chords, 'as of a thousand Eolian harps'. Angels are considered to be a class of spirits who are devoted to music and who habitually express themselves this way. Late one night in the pub Alicia heard just such a sound. "I knew the radio was off. When I walked by the radio speakers I could hear music coming from them. It was the most heavenly music I have ever heard."

Is Alicia a sensitive? "When I was a child my grandmother died. About two weeks after her death I was sleeping with my mother when I suddenly awakened. Apparently my dead grandmother had appeared and walked to the bedside where my mother was laying. My mother's arm was hanging over the side of the bed. My grandmother took my mother's hand and held it. Then she moved back towards the wall and disappeared."

If a mother is a 'sensitive', her daughter may have the same abilities. Similarly, mothers and daughters can have a deep psychic bond. Energy and psychic awareness are often awakened when one dies. When the physical body goes and only energy remains, some of that energy may be gifted by the mother to her daughter, a true psychic legacy.

The many and varied accounts of spiritual activity in the building would seem to indicate that several spirits inhabit Cherry Hill House. There is activity in the attic and in the office located at the base of the attic staircase. Customers have seen a spirit on the main floor, as well as the pub. Several different spirits have been seen including the white figure rising up out of the earth brandishing a sword, a girl wearing white riding a horse inside the building, a tall native man wearing buckskins in the pub, an old native man appearing in the attic, a native girl standing by the fireplace on the first floor of the restaurant, a hissing cat and the sound of heavenly music, which may indicate a higher order of spirit. Spiritualists claim that the sound of angelic music or the sweet scent of flowers indicates a visitation from a higher dimension of spirit beings. They include angels and saints who are not caught on this plane but are attendant here to help those who need them.

This is a lot of activity for one building; did William Romain make some kind of spirit corridor here when he invited spirits in through his seances? You may judge for yourself when you visit the Cherry Hill Restaurant.

Time Travellers

The day was sunny and the waters calm when a young couple headed out boating along the jagged rocky shoreline of Newfoundland. Their destination was a small fishing hamlet located a few miles to the south. Everything seemed fine. However, their perception was soon altered when a low fog bank began to roll in and the light quickly faded to grey. Minutes turned into hours and fearing the worst they wondered it they would simply pass the village without ever seeing it and vanish from sight. Just when all seemed lost they saw it. A light shining in the window of a house up on top of a bluff. They headed towards the light and found the channel that brought them in. When they docked they quickly related their story and the gratitude they felt for the light in the window. Blank stares soon revealed the truth. According to the locals the house they had seen had burned down several years before and all that was left to mark the site was a foundation and a couple of grave stones nearby. Had they, indeed, stepped into the fourth dimension?

We call the fourth dimension time. For the most part people are unfamiliar with even the thought of 'stepping outside of time'. Others are actually unaware that they are experiencing anything out of the ordinary when in fact they are in an altered time reality. There are no gauges to help us here, no rules of the game. In time travel, it is simply a shift to another plane of consciousness and perception. This is where the present no longer exists and the past comes to life.

A person never sees oneself in time. Maurice Nicoll writes in PSYCHOLOGICAL COMMENTARIES ON THE TEACHING OF G.I. GURDJIEFF AND OUSPENSKY, "We do not see the Time-Bodies of ourselves or of things. We think the past is dead. Our lives are living lines in living Time. Owing to our relation to Time, however, we see only a point in Time and then another, and we call them present moments."

In our physical life we are conscious of three dimensions of space—length, height and depth or volume. What we don't see are other dimensions. For that we need the power of astral sight. To be able to see beyond the blindfold of beliefs and enter the world some people call the 'illusion'.

In the fourth dimension objects and inhabitants are real in the same way as our own bodies, our furniture, our houses or monuments. All we need to do is shed our perceived concept of time. We need to rid ourselves of the clock and function according to solar time. Think about dreams for a moment. During a dream we have no concept of time. A full 'video' can happen in a few minutes of ordinary time. We simply travel to wherever our dreams take us. When we wake up we have no recollection of time. Where did we go and for how long?

This veil of time appears quite thin in many places, par-

Time travellers

ticularly in specific natural settings. Native elders have long eluded to these sacred places and called them portals. Most people are too uncomfortable to share any time experience for fear of ridicule. However, Ian Mollet was more than willing to share with us.

Ian is a soft-spoken man who has lived his life in balance with the great outdoors. At the early age of five he would hunker down in a hand- fashioned fort in old furs while the wind howled around it. There he dreamed of other times when men and women faced the elements and lived in simple ways. He believes he was once a coureur de bois.

His great-great-grandfather settled in Canada in the 1860s. This man died at the age of 89 but he had been a visionary, knowing there would be wars and depressions.

"I have been a trailblazer since the age of five. That was when I made my first trail in the bush." Ian has the instinctive gift of finding direction without the aid of compass, sun, moon or stars. He can look at a map and then begin to travel from point A and arrive at point B without any navigational aids.

Ian has another gift. He is able to enter the fourth dimension and travel back to another time. His first clear recollection of this was an incident that occurred while on a canoe and fishing trip on the French River back in the early 1980s in the month of June. Keep in mind this river was a major fur trading route in the 17th and 18th centuries. Ian and a group of father/son and father/daughter teams had rented some rustic cabins near Noelville by the French River. At about 5:00 p.m. one day Ian and his good friend, Ron, decided to canoe a short distance west of the cabins to a high rock on the south shore of the French. Pulling up to shore they disembarked and began to climb the eight metre ascent (24 feet) to the top. The view was spectacular. The men could see the river in both directions. A few cabins dotted the shoreline.

"We were sitting side by side on the rock. In tune and comfortable with one another, we sat there contemplating our own private thoughts. While I was sitting there a peculiar wave-like action happened to my vision. It was like a wind coming up on a body of calm water, causing the water to ripple. Suddenly the buildings along the river disappeared. The trees and the river remained. I was back in the 1600s and I was indeed a coureur de bois. We were on our way to Georgian Bay. I was no longer aware of Ron. The configuration of the river was slightly different and the water was moving much faster. Then this ripple effect occurred again to my vision and I came back wondering what the hell had just happened. Ron knew something was up and I explained it all to him as best I could."

Ian didn't have another experience like this until the early 1990s when he and his wife were on the cruise ship out of Parry Sound. "We had just left the dock when this wave action happened again to my vision. At the time we were looking across the harbour at the Sound Marina and the houses along the shoreline. Once again everything disappeared. I was back in the early 1600s. All the houses were gone and the forest touched the waters' edge."

Ian has had other experiences of the paranormal. In 1983 he was in a hockey dressing room talking to some people when something very unusual happened to him. "I disappeared. I could hear the peoples' conversation, but I was above them. My body no longer existed. I was really above and beyond myself watching people having a conversation that only a few moments before I had been part of."

Ian was also close to his father who passed away in 1992. He hoped to see him in his dreams but little did he expect what he got!

In 1997 he left work at lunch hour and proceeded to the Georgian Inn to work out in their gym. This was quite a common practice for Ian. As he walked downstairs and into the small change room he sensed he was not alone.

"I turned around to take my shirt off and caught my reflection in the wall mirror. My face was my Father's face. I felt the familiar wavy action occur with my vision. There I was looking at my Father. I knew as long as I maintained eye contact with him he would remain. It seemed as though he wanted to relate something to me. His face was so calm. I got the feeling he was consoling me. Why was it going on so long? It was like watching something on video going from one segment to the other. When I glanced away he was gone."

A short time later Ian was diagnosed with chronic lymphatic leukemia. He is still battling this today with all his remarkable physical and spiritual strength.

Ian had more yet to share. He looked down a moment and then recalled his meditation classes in the 1980s.

"One night I was sitting on the edge of my bed meditating before going to sleep. Meditation helps me to prepare myself for a good night's sleep. It was when I was saying certain affirmations to myself that I had the feeling that my mind wanted to take me somewhere. I decided to go with it. All of a sudden I was north of Mono Centre on the Bruce Trail at the highest point in the area on an open-crowned hill. I was looking down the valley viewing ponds and cliffs and trees. I was sitting on a rock and beside me was a friend whom I have known since I was ten years old. This friend would not normally be in the Bruce Trail area. He is a very devout Catholic and has very strong beliefs. I looked at my friend and said to him, 'This is my God', while holding my hands out to the valley below. Immediately after I spoke, I levitated off the ground above him and started to fly very slowly down the valley. I was about 350 metres (400 yards) above the ground.

"I remember heading south and then I started to accelerate. As I gained altitude I swung out through the stratosphere and into deep space. Now the planets and the stars began to whiz by me. I continued to go until I left this galaxy. I wondered where I was heading. I came not to darkness nor to brightness. It was a palpable gray that soon became light and then I came to a full stop. I was at the centre of everything. Far more than any time in my life before or since I knew there was a God. I also immediately understood and knew everything I needed to know. About time, I knew at that point, that the past, the future and the present were one; I knew the history of the world; I could understand the teachings of love; I could forgive people like Hitler for what they did; I knew it was right to forgive; I felt happy to have realized that. Then it happened. The whole experience overwhelmed me. My mind could not handle the experience. I became frightened. I came reeling back to the side of the bed. My heart was pounding. What had just taken place?

"In that moment I was like an encyclopedia of knowledge concerning the history of mankind. I did not know what to do. The logical thing was to crawl into bed. I lay there with my eyes wide open. I woke up my wife, Pam, and described the entire experience to her. Then I felt much calmer. I sensed real peace for the first time in my life.

"For the next several days I maintained a working and living lifestyle that reflected this knowledge of forgiveness and acceptance. People began to respond positively to me. Ultimately, however, the enlightenment wore thin. I have tried many times to get back to that special place but each time I have failed. I am still waiting."

Ian Mollett is not alone. Others, like Ian, have experienced extraordinary journeys in time. It takes a kind of sensitivity to be open to the experience of ghosts. Here is a man who has experienced his father as a ghost and also, in a way, himself.

Claudette Boyd, owner of Health Connections, a bookstore and alternative health counselling centre in Parry Sound, had an experience she related to me. One night a stranger came knocking at her door and Claudette filled more than a few pages in her journal when she left.

"It was eight o'clock on a Sunday night in April. I heard a knock at the front door. A lady was standing on my doorstep. She said to me, 'I was just out to get some milk at the store and for some reason I knew I had to stop here and see if anyone was home'."

She needed to talk to someone. Apparently she had heard about Claudette but had never met her before. This stranger had arrived on her doorstep because she had a story to tell and was searching for some answers.

"I sat down and listened to her. She began by telling me about an archeological dig that took place near Collingwood. Apparently, someone had found an ancient native village. Her husband was associated with the archaeologist on the site and together they had decided to visit the dig. When they went to the site she experienced a different time.

"She was suddenly a young woman sitting in a circle of Native elders, including a medicine man. She also saw that she lived in the village near this medicine man. She was close to this holy man and appeared to be happy.

"She was married to a young brave who was killed in battle. This medicine man knew this was going to happen but did nothing to prevent it. She discovered this and had come to hate the medicine man. Suddenly she knew she was back in the present with her husband. He was aware that something had happened to her. She did not want to leave the area. She knew she could return to that time at any moment. Her husband sensed her distress, walked her to their car and took her out for ice cream! He placed a cone in her hand and that seemed to jolt her back to reality.

"Two years later she had a deep yearning to return to the site. Her husband had died and she had too many unanswered questions. She followed the same pathway and came to the spot where she had stepped into altered time. Thorny bushes now blocked the entry point. Suddenly she received the message not to go back.

"She remembered the first time when the medicine man had spoken directly to her. He had told her why he had not tried to prevent her young husband's death. She understood what he was saying but still felt anger towards him."

"What do I do with this experience?" she asked Claudette. "What does it all mean?"

Was this woman still carrying anger from another lifetime? Why could she not go back a second time? How does someone cope with such an experience? Who would believe her?

The experience was real to her. Certainly a message was delivered and she heard it. Perhaps this is why she could not return a second time. The difficulty is in believing that it has actually happened and then in finding someone to listen to your story and help you to understand its meaning.

A ghost appears in the present but comes from the past. If we travel back in time do we become a ghost of the future? When a ghost is attached to a person and travels with them wherever they go what does that say about space? Ottilie Hubmann has a forty-year personal haunting to share.

Ottilie is quite a remarkable person. She is awake in this lifetime. Her earliest memory is from the age of six months, lying in a wicker basket listening to her older brother crying. She remembers thinking, "Why is he so worried?" It was war time, and Ottilie's parents had abandoned their children in Munich, Germany. They were alone.

Her next strong memory was at the age of two when she had the thought,

"Why am I here in an orphanage? I don't belong here!" Shortly afterwards she was adopted.

A childhood experience has been her life-long guiding light. She explains, "When I was four years old, living with stepparents, I remember standing in front of a large mirror in the entranceway and looking at myself and asking 'Who am I?' I knew at that moment that I could just go. I was not limited to the physical body. I could leave this body at any time. At that moment I remembered I am spirit, not body. I still get goose bumps relating this story. I was searching for the spiritual. I think an experience like this is important to you. It helps to lead the way."

Being open to spirit also allows you to see what others cannot. As a young girl Ottilie recalls lying in bed and seeing the shadow of a body out of the corner of her eye. She also saw sparks in the air. At 16 she came face to face with this shadow. It was a frightening and shocking experience for one who was so young, innocent and quite alone with the experience.

"At age 16 I was still living in Munich. I was very shy and innocent. It was in the morning in my bedroom when I woke up to a man standing at the entrance to my room. He was of average height wearing a black, hooded cloak and brandishing a knife. The only part you could see of his face were his lips. They were bright red. As he approached me, he suddenly vanished into thin air. He appeared to be quite vicious."

This black-cloaked figure would only appear when Ottilie was experiencing some stress and always in her bedroom. In the first year he appeared five times. Sometimes he even seemed as though he wanted to strangle her.

At age 23 she left Munich for South Africa. She sighed a sense of relief knowing she would never see this hideous figure that had haunted her youth. "I moved to a place with a large bay window. One morning I awoke to a dazzling sunrise. All of a sudden I saw a pair of hands opening the window from the outside. I froze with fear. This was a bad dream. He was back. I watched him climb through the window and approach my bed. Then he disappeared.

"I didn't know what to do. I couldn't talk to anyone. He always appeared in the morning. Sometimes he came through the window and other times through the doorway. He never spoke a word. I always felt evil. He never walked through a wall. He was as real as you or I."

Three years later Ottilie moved back to Germany and he followed her once again. As a matter of fact, each time she moved, he moved. There was nothing she could do, it was inevitable that he would 'show up'.

In 1982 she moved to Parry Sound with her husband. Within the first month he appeared. It would seem this spirit had no problem crossing continents. This time, however, he came much closer to her. "He was about 1.5 metres (four feet) from me. I saw his eyes. They were quite normal-looking. Finally I had enough. I shouted at him 'Go, I am not afraid of you. I don't want to see you anymore'. It worked, he disappeared and I never saw him again. That is until the late 1980's when I had decided to travel to New

Mexico to a conference on past-life regression.

I wanted to know what my soul's journey was. For the first few days at the conference in New Mexico we meditated and each worked with a facilitator. One day I told my facilitator that I was feeling quite depressed. This is quite unusual since I am always a very happy person. I felt like I had a black cloud hovering over me. My facilitator said maybe we had something here. He had me lay down and he stood behind me. He told me that when I breathed in I was to ask for a symbol.

"The symbol I saw for myself was a ballpoint pen. I was disappointed. After all, they didn't have ballpoint pens in the past. How could this be a symbol for my higher self? However, I followed the instructions and soon a picture appeared. I was in a chamber in a castle. It was a torture chamber. Here comes my bad past I thought. I was the victim.

"My facilitator wanted to close the session after relating this to him. Yet, I really believed something was about to happen. We kept going. Then he appeared. The black-cloaked figure, who I had not seen in a number of years. He was in the torture chamber with me holding a book open in one hand and a quill pen in the other. There was my symbol, the ballpoint pen. I could feel him and I knew everything that he was thinking. This was the man who was responsible for signing my death warrant. He was feeling guilty that he had not saved my life. He had become emotionally attached to me.

"We then sent him love. Please go to the light. I took his hand and we walked to the light. Go on to the light. He entered the light and disappeared. I knew he was gone for good."

Ottilie has not seen him since but he was certainly with her for many years.

—⁓—

Each of these three stories seemed like an illusion to the participant. However, Ian Mollett did in fact see the landscape change in front of him. When he looked into the mirror his face did become his Father's face. Was it just a coincidence that Ian became ill with cancer shortly afterwards? And what about his journey during meditation when Ian stepped outside of time and shifted to another plane of insight? It was real enough to change his outlook on life.

The woman at Claudette's door needed to tell her story. She needed someone to believe her. The time portal she entered is one well-known to Native elders. Was it a coincidence that her husband knew the archaeologist? Native peoples have always connected with their ancestors to help them make present-day decisions that will affect their tomorrows. Visions of past events are part of that Sacred medicine.

Ottilie Hubmann's early childhood memories certainly indicate an aware spirit.

How do we unlock the mystery of time, the movement of the fourth dimension of reality? When does it come to each person's aid? What beacons of light have any of us had and not recognized as 'out of ordinary time'? Have we found other ways to explain them or have we suppressed them out of fear?

Legg's General Store, Birr

I have given this place heart and soul for 25 years. Things were in need of change and I followed my spirit. I've always been a fan of the Civil War, especially of General McPherson. He was a northerner, but beloved by both armies and he was killed in battle. I realized that he died too young, his life uncompleted. When you work in the public eye there is both happiness and grief in abundance."

Meet Jack Legg, proprietor of Legg's General Store in Birr, Ontario near London. A deep and abstract thinker, Jack equates the history of General McPherson to the trials and tribulations of today. He is a sensitive man with a gift for touching others in a special way even as he was touched in a special way by General McPherson's unfinished life.

His store is a serendipitous adventure, a warehouse of eclectic surprises designed to touch the hearts of anyone and everyone who enters therein. Jack sells almost everything including: books, Mexican glassware, toys, candy, giftware, Mennonite furniture, homespun sweaters, flowers, plants, nursery stock, statuary, firewood, candles, incense, food and numerous other items. His general store is experiential, not to mention magical. No one leaves empty-handed or empty-headed. Jack's passion is his understanding of the past and he loves to share his philosophy with interested customers.

"He (General McPherson) gives me the strength to do anything. I can battle despair or war, I can handle it; if there is an emergency, I can handle it. There is no heaven or hell, it's how you live that counts, how you honour it. I have no fear of dying. Living is the difficult thing."

Jack's interest in General McPherson and his life is unusual. Has that interest actually drawn the spirit of General McPherson to him or is there some other reason he has appeared on Jack's property?

The Native American way is to not mention a person's name once they are deceased; to speak their name is to call them back. Instead the person would be referred to by title, such as 'grandmother', 'mother' or 'daughter'. Do Jack's thoughts and conversations about General McPherson call him back and keep him there?

General McPherson first appeared in 1993. "I saw these riding boots and blue trousers down the alley between two outbuildings. I knew it had to be something. Time in this dimension has no minutes or hours." Jack is convinced it was General McPherson. There was a tavern next door at one time that was frequented by the Donnellys whose spirits are still restless in the district. In HAUNTED ONTARIO, I referred to the night of February 3, 1880, when a group of men arrived at the Donnelly homestead, a few miles away from Birr, and savagely beat several family members to death. The hotel once located next door to Jack's General Store was a stagecoach stop and stomping ground for the Donnellys.

Tom Donnelly, the son of James and Johannah, was not always welcome at the hotel. George Swartz, the hotel proprietor quoted in the Huron Expositor newspaper stated, "One day Thomas Donnelly sat in the bar, somewhat under the influence of liquor, when he carelessly pulled a revolver from his pocket, pointed the muzzle over his shoulder and fired, regardless of the consequences. The bullet passed uncomfortably close to Mr. Swartz's head, burying itself in the wall. Donnelly then fired another shot, with as much nonchalance, which lodged in the ceiling."

Tom was later stabbed repeatedly with a pitchfork and clubbed outside the Donnelly homestead on the night of the murders. His body was eventually dragged back inside the house where his skull was laid open with a shovel.

There are ghosts at their homestead and perhaps Tom is still hoping for a drink—or maybe revenge. The spirit on the property was not seen until after the hotel came down in 1964. Is that just a coincidence or could the 'presence' be a Donnelly ? Or are there two spirits?

Although only visible from the legs down, Jack has no doubt that the spirit is General McPherson. Somehow Jack's journey is interwoven with this Civil War General, born James Birdseye McPherson on November 4, 1828, in Sandusky County, Ohio. McPherson was a man who grew up in extreme poverty. It's quite ironic that it was a storekeeper, like Jack, who helped McPherson secure an appointment to West Point from which he graduated in 1853 at the head of his class.

Major General William T. Sherman repeatedly used McPherson's army to outflank strong Confederate defense lines. On July 22, 1864, McPherson attempted to repeat the success when General John B. Hood delivered a surprise counterattack southeast of Atlanta. McPherson decided to ride forward to investigate. To his surprise he encountered a force of Confederates, who shot and killed him as he tried to retreat. At the time of his death General Ulysses S. Grant is reported to have said, "The country has lost one of its best soldiers, and I have lost my best friend."

Coincidentally, Jack's mother's family was from Michigan and lived there at the time of the Civil War. The state of Michigan played an active role during the war against the Confederates as did London, Ontario, and the district including Birr. Orlo Miller, author of LONDON, states, "The American Civil War had a deep and lasting effect on the history of Canada, and nowhere was it felt more strongly than in London. The North stood for paid labour, the South for slave labour. The North represented the working man, the South, the Establishment."

Miller also points out, "The economic picture had changed rapidly. The farmers of the western part of the province of Ontario had greeted the outbreak of the Civil War with some enthusiasm, expecting an increased demand for their wheat." The agricultural development of Kansas soon met the demand but the Northern armies required beef. Canadian farmers immediately responded by supplying the army with meat. During the Civil War many new farmhouses in the London area were built by beef barons.

The northern armies also required volunteers to fight the South. Many Canadians living in Ontario who had relatives in the northern states left to join the Northern Forces.

Legg's General Store

Many never returned.

It was rumoured that gold was hidden somewhere in the hotel next to the general store. Jack said, "Apparently someone back in 1854 had stopped in for a drink and mentioned he was going to buy some land in the area. He even admitted to having the money to buy it. That night he was rolled for his money. However, the stranger's money never surfaced. The culprit had the gold coins in the keg room of the tavern on a ledge. Unfortunately for the thief, the box containing the coins fell behind the ledge and disappeared."

Jack took over the business from his father in 1967. His father had purchased the property in 1947. Jack Sr. was a very generous man. He operated an extensive business which included dry goods, a lumber mill and a grist mill. Jack compares his dad's business to an Eaton's store. Whatever people needed you could bet Jack Sr. stocked it. He was also known for his generosity—he fed anyone who arrived on his premises hungry.

In 1964 Jack Senior decided to demolish the building. It was while removing some floor boards that he discovered a box containing six gold coins. The hidden treasure had been found. The discovery of coins was to have a profound effect on Jack Junior. Today, Jack knows the power of gifting by way of coins.

In the course of running his general store Jack encounters numerous people from all walks of life. He can sense the tragedy that touches many. "I've been a lucky fellow. I collect some of the coins that come into the store and put them on a shelf near the front counter."

Jack offers these coins to bring people good luck. When

he meets someone in despair he hands them a coin. "I hope you take this with you." To the amazement of the person something good usually happens to them. Jack's gift of coins is a gift in many ways.

"A lady once came into the store for some mint chocolates. I said I didn't have any. She then told me about a tragic snowmobile accident that had happened in front of her house. Two young boys were travelling down the road and collided with a vehicle. She felt responsible because it happened in front of her home. I gave her a coin. Then she disappeared.

"Two weeks later a different woman came in the store and thanked me for giving the coin to her son. There were tears in her eyes as she said, 'I want you to meet him.' The son was suffering from a severe head injury. He shook my hand and thanked me for this lucky coin. Apparently he was to have surgery, but ended up not needing it. I had no idea how this woman obtained the coin. My wife was a witness to all this. Then I began to wonder who the woman was who had come in two weeks earlier worried about a snowmobile accident in front of her home. She had to be an angel. How else would this other woman have received one of my coins?"

There is no question that Legg's General Store is haunted and there is no question that Jack Legg can see and feel more than most. Does his spirit- friend inspire some of his insight? Is it a special sensitivity he has or is it a place where the separation of a dimension is not so pronounced. The energy there is very different. I feel that the longer I linger the more likely I am to be surprised by a spirit.

"Is a man a lighthouse?" Jack asked me. He asks many odd-seeming questions like that; he expresses himself in images, often jarring and not immediately relevant to the conversation. Who or what is prompting him?

This particular question opened the door for me to understand Jack Legg. 'Is a man a lighthouse?' Jack is! General McPherson was! They shine a light, set an example, gift a coin, ask a surprise question or make an unusual statement; they are spirits, expressing the moment, one more visible than the other. If I were to be haunted by a spirit I would certainly choose to have it an inspirational haunting like the one in Birr. Don't drive on by; stop in for a snack, a gift, a moment of philosophy and, perhaps, a sighting.

Mylar and Loreta's Singhampton

A woman stands at the entranceway beckoning you to come forward. Her greeting reminds you of something long forgotten. The furnishings in the room nudge a memory, a savory secret. You are seated at a table with a flickering candle; a menu appears in your hand; your first glance yields the Legend of Mylar and Loreta:

T"was 100 years ago or so that Mylar left his home
To find his fame and fortune, in the new land he would roam.
His journey was a long one. But finally he found
A home here in Singhampton, with good friends all around.

He talked of a fair lady, the finest in his land
And when the time was ready, he wrote home for her hand.
Loreta's heart was bursting, her stately ship set sail
The sky was bright, the sea was calm, no thought of stormy gale.

Then came that night of terror when her ship went down at sea.
Her soul released to Heaven, her spirit was set free.
Some say she came to Mylar, it is difficult to know.
His love for her kept growing. He could never let her go.

Now as you sit and dine today and enjoy our country inn
Feel the power of their special love that lingers from within.

Could this tale be true—if you're a ghost hunter your heart skips a beat at this point. If your curiosity compels you to question you will discover that a spirit has actually taken up residence here among the living, in this stylish old hotel now converted to a restaurant and pub.

A ghost was discovered at the Inn and to explain its existence the tale of Mylar and Loreta was invented. The employees call their resident ghost, Mylar, in keeping with the story, and now fact and fiction remain entwined.

The main street of historic Singhampton is the locale of this period hotel from the 1860s. The town itself is located in the township of Osprey in the eastern part of Grey County on the 400 metre (1,200 foot) high plateau of the Blue Mountains. Its origins date back to the 1840s when Josiah R. Sing arrived.

Settlement was slow, the climate unpredictable. Growth came from mills on the local Mad River and the community actually once bore the name of "Mad River Mills". Eventually named after it's founder, Josiah Sing, Singhampton literally translates to Sing's Town.

Lumbermen required housing and hotels filled the bill. Singhampton actually had two hotels located side by side on the main street. The first brick tavern to be built in Singhampton was in the early 1850s. The business provided accommodation for travelers, land speculators and survey crews who came to the district. A second hotel, now Mylar and Loreta's, was constructed sometime in the late 1850s. The first hotel was called the Lower Hotel. John Stinson owned and operated it until 1865 when it was renamed Stinson's Tavern. Sometime later the name changed to

Victoria Inn. It provided housing for horses as well as people and served meals and liquid refreshments from 10:00 a.m. to 3:00 p.m, primarily to hungry lumbermen. The Upper Hotel, as the other one was known, had a great series of names: the Royal Hotel, the Blackstock Hotel, the Exchange Hotel, the Hampton House and, ultimately, Mylar and Loreta's.

By 1919 fishermen had discovered Singhampton and they arrived from Toronto by train to fish in the trout-filled streams and rivers. They came for a weekend, a week, or maybe took a room for a month. Singhampton was a tourist mecca. In the 1930s the first May weekend brought more than 30 men to each hotel.

In 1984 Sandy Spencer purchased the business. Fate played a hand—a kick in the backside makes all the difference in the world. Sandy, an energetic and self-motivated woman, had been living in Collingwood where she worked as a manager in a busy restaurant. "Why not own your own business if you're going to work so hard!" She thought one day. Sandy was raising two young children and had recently lost her mother. There was a void in her life. She knew she needed a focus.

Her fate brought her to the auction sale of the Hampton Hotel. Could she really afford it? Was this what she was truly meant to do?

On the morning of the auction, Sandy decided to sleep in—the auction momentarily forgotten. Not to be! Sandy was startled from her sleep by a kick to the backside. "Who kicked me?" she thought. No one was there. She noticed the time and decided forthwith to get up and attend that auction with her three-year-old son. She will never forget that day! The auctioneer cried, "Do I hear a bid?" Lo and behold, her young son raised his hand. Her son was, of course, not registered, so she was given the opportunity to decline the bid. But that was it. Sandy honoured the bid. She now owned The Hampton Hotel. She had no idea, however, that the place was haunted!

Anne is a kind, middle-aged woman who also finds her fate connected to the old hotel. She has worked in the building for 19 years. Anne and Sandy had never met until Sandy purchased the property. On the same morning when Sandy was kicked in bed by a spirit, Anne also experienced something unusual.

"The morning Sandy was kicked I was sound asleep in bed. I remember waking up when someone or something kicked me in the back. I didn't even know who Sandy Spencer was."

Sandy said, "My mother had recently passed away. I believe it was my mother who kicked me in bed, trying to tell me to get up and go to the auction." Was it?

Did Sandy's mother have her eye on Anne as well? Sandy was going to need help with her new undertaking and her mother must have been aware of that fact. Sandy met Anne and hired her. It was Anne who told her about the spirit who appears in certain places in the building. But Sandy soon experienced an encounter of her own.

"One day I was cleaning the tables in the dining room area. I looked up and there was a man looking at me. Then he disappeared. He was tall and slender and he wore a red plaid shirt and denim overalls. It looked like he was wearing a straw hat. He appeared to be middle-aged. He was standing right in front of the kitchen doors just by the dining room entrance."

As you enter the front door of the establishment you walk a short distance before you reach the main entranceway to the restaurant. Straight ahead are the kitchen doors. To your left is a spacious dining room. To your right is a quaint, cozy bar with an opening behind for wait staff to place orders to the kitchen. Wooden stools line the bar. The furnishings are old and eclectic and reflect the many periods that this place has known.

Mylar has been seen seated at the bar on the stool on the far right. Perhaps he is waiting for a drink.

One night at about 10:30 p.m., when Sandy was alone in the restaurant, Mylar appeared. "I was busy behind the bar when I saw him peering at me through the small opening to the kitchen. I thought for a moment 'Who is this guy?' Then he vanished. I went to look but no one was there. I can never make out his face.

"Another time a customer in the hallway saw a man standing at the sideboard located on the right hand side. The man was pulling out a drawer. That was one customer I lost. She swore he closed the drawer before he disappeared. I have no idea what he was looking for."

One day the cook and another employee saw a man in a red plaid shirt standing at the back door. They asked him if they could help him and he disappeared in front of them.

It would seem that Mylar is fond of table-settings. Cutlery in the dining area was moved so often the staff started to keep watch on the room. The cutlery would be reversed at a table setting. Kitchen items also went missing. Sandy mused, "Too bad he doesn't clean!"

Sandy feels the spirit is lost on this plane, an earthbound soul. She has often talked to him about finding the light. No one knows who he is. Sandy has a feeling or intuitive hunch he was a frequent visitor to the hotel in the 1920s and 1930s. One thing is certain. Mylar relates to Anne. He has appeared to her on numerous occasions over the last 19 years. Her first sighting was many years ago in the dining room. She thought she had seen a customer standing at the entranceway of the dining room by the kitchen doors. "I went toward him and he vanished. On another occasion I was in the dining room and I heard my name called. It was a male voice. No one was there.

"I believe he is a friendly soul. I have never been frightened of him. He looks like a farmer. He stands about 2 metres (6' 2") tall and has a slim build.

"One night our cook was cleaning up after the restaurant had closed. There were no customers in the building. She looked out the kitchen doors and saw Mylar sitting at the far end of the bar on a stool. Then he disappeared.

"Last fall a traveller stopped in for something to eat. She told me she was a healer. As soon as she stepped in the door she said there is a spirit here man. She had dinner and left."

Spirits are often attracted to individuals who are 'sensitive'. When Anne was asked if she had ever had any early experiences with spirits she nodded. "When I was nine years old I lived in Simcoe. I remember I was in my bedroom and curled up in bed with a magazine. Suddenly the pages started to turn on their own. That was strange and yet it didn't really frighten me. I realized it might have been the young girl who died in a fire in the basement before we owned the house."

Anne paused a moment and recalled another experience with her mother. "I was living in Delhi in a Victorian farmhouse with my parents. I was always terrified of staying alone in that place. My mother often said an older man, a spirit, would be seen walking through the house and the attic. She once told me he had spoken to her. He said, 'Tell your daughter not to be afraid. I am looking after her'.

Perhaps he is still looking after her. Maybe he even kicked her in bed!

When asked why she has worked so long in one place, she replies, "This is my extended family." She is, of course, including Mylar.

Mylar is seen at the back door of the kitchen and at the entranceway of the dining room. Although he is held responsible for moving cutlery in the restaurant, he has never been seen in the room. Mylar seems to like to sit at the bar and also to poke his head through the kitchen opening. Seems he's quite 'at home', opening drawers and moving things about, looking for God knows what.

Overalls, plaid shirt, straw hat, Mylar could have been a local farmer waiting for his beloved to arrive.

One thing you can count on at Mylar and Loretas, you'll never have to dine alone.

The Ottawa International Hostel & Carleton County Gaol

Out of the shower and into the change room. The clothes have vanished. In the hallway a sock appears, a shirt...pants...belt...underwear, scattered down the hall like stepping stones. Where is the watch!?! The search begins in another room or, more accurately put, another cell. No longer ticking, the watch lies upside down on a cold, concrete floor. The searcher flees to his room. What on earth just took place? There are common occurrences for those who stay in the Ottawa International Hostel, once the Carleton County Gaol. Time stops on Death Row.

In this building, literally hundreds of lost souls wander the corridors, up and down the stairwells, occupying cells, remaining on death row, waiting, waiting, waiting. A noose was always hanging from the gallows, swinging like a pendulum, marking time. Each time it stopped, another unmarked grave was dug in the dusty courtyard. Reports written by the Inspector of Jails in the 1870s bares witness to the atrocities.

Children cried out. Women wept. Men prayed for their souls as the jailor turned the key. Darkness would blanket the lost and forsaken and smother their torment. A woman dragged into a secret passageway was assaulted. Her cries were muffled. She prayed for it to end. In total darkness naked people were sentenced to six months 'in the hole', spread-eagled and chained to a cold cell floor to die without seeing daylight again. What prompted such cruelty?

In 1862 the Carleton County Gaol opened as a maximum security holding facility. Many people were actually innocent victims, men, women and children. Once incarcerated they were seldom allowed to shower, never given more than one meal a day, never saw daylight and died in filthy, unlit quarters in the basement, known as the quarantine area. When they died their bodies were burned in the courtyard. Other victims were illegally hung inside the building, far from the view of any governing officials.

Many people died here as a result of societal prejudice against the mentally ill and the poor, and methods of treatment that resulted from this prejudice. To declare a person insane was one such method. The fate of many unfortunate victims rested in the hands of jailers and inspectors of jails. In August of 1876 Inspector Christie observed the following, "I found 58 prisoners in custody, 31 males and 27 females. Of the women, 25 were under sentence, one waiting trial and one, Mary McLoughlin, was insane. She appeared to be a fit subject for asylum treatment."

A common example of punishment is recorded in Inspector J.W. Langmuir's report dated September 24, 1877, "Reference has again to be made to the case of Margaret Dogherty, who, owing to outrageous conduct, has constantly to be kept under punishment, being at this time tied to the cell door. Although, properly speaking, the woman may not be insane, there can be no doubt she is a fit subject for an asylum. Sarah Jane Thomas has not yet been certified to be a lunatic and at the time of my visit appeared to be quite sane, although was evidently of weak intelligence."

The Carleton County Gaol closed in 1972 because of lack of sanitation, poor lighting and unsavory conditions. In 1973 the building became the Ottawa International Hostel. Portions of the interior were renovated to accommodate overnight guests but much of the jail remains as it was, including the cell blocks, the gallows, the hole, the stairwells, the secret tunnels and death row.

Wade Kirkpatrick is the friendly Operations Manager of the hostel. Although Wade has never seen a ghost he has experienced unexplained activity. "My wife, Crystal, and I lived here for four months before we bought our first house. We lived in an apartment on the seventh floor. We often heard voices and banging on the pipes, although no one was to be seen. People often claim to hear cell doors closing behind them as they walk down death row, which is on the floor above the apartment. One time we went away for a week and shut the water off to our apartment. When we returned from our holidays the water was turned on and hot water was now coming out of the cold water tap."

Guided tours of the building are offered. Carol Devine, one of the tour guides, discusses its history, its mystery and the hauntings of the jail. I joined Carol on her tour. Come along.

It began in the basement. Carol usually does not take a group here because it is nerve-racking. A set of stairs leads down to a room that has the appearance of a black hole. The lights were not working. It was chilling and oppressive. This area had been used as a quarantine station for newly-arrived immigrants in the mid-1860s who were thought to be suffering from scarlet fever. In most cases the whole family would be sentenced to the basement of the Carleton County Gaol for no less than three months.

Carol said, "This is where thousands of people died. Whole families would be shoved into this space and left to fend for themselves. Most of the jail guards were afraid to enter the area for fear of catching the disease. I assume their honey buckets (pails that served as toilets) were never removed or cleaned, but rather were dumped in the corner of the room. When residents died, the guards would remove their bodies and burn them in the back courtyard. No one ever received a proper burial."

On we went to Debtors' Prison. People who could not afford to pay their bills were impounded here. They were sentenced to work in the kitchen and other areas of the jail. Many came with their families who were housed in dormitory-style cells. This section of the building was converted to a chapel shortly after 1920, when Canada abolished such prisons.

Down the hallway there is an entranceway to a tunnel which leads to the courthouse next door. Part of the tunnel has been filled in. Carol remarked, "People hear moaning coming from the tunnel. I am certain prisoners were taken down into the tunnel and abused. No one would ever hear their screams." A door seals the sight but not the sounds!

Next, Station 2, Solitary Confinement, nicknamed 'The

Hole'. Six cells were used to house troublesome inmates and they remain intact to this day. Here inmates were placed for one day to six months. All privileges, including visitors, exercise, and chapel, were taken away. Prisoners were forced to use honeybuckets instead of toilets. The cells had two doors. The second door was made of solid wood, and no light came through. Prisoners were often stripped of their clothing and shackled, spread-eagled, on the floor. Once a day the guard would unchain them for 15 minutes to eat their only meal and to use the honeybucket. Many inmates died in that darkness. The unlit cells and shackles are still as they were. The suffering in that room is palpable. Scratch marks are visible on the walls and floors.

At one end of solitary confinement is "A" and "D", now also referred to as Station 3, where the admittance and departure of inmates took place. Here prisoners were stripped of their clothes and personal belongings, taken to the shower, given prison clothing, tobacco, a comb and a toothbrush without a handle. This is now a kitchen!

Station 4 was originally the visiting area. There are metal screens on the staircase that act as anti-suicide bars. They run up the entire staircase. Although not often actually seen, a spirit haunts this area. The 'presence' follows visitors up the stairs and imposes pressure from behind. In 1910 two inmates overpowered a guard and threw him to his death in this stairwell. A menacing presence has remained. I experienced it very strongly.

Station 5 was originally cellblock one and two and is now a residence for female visitors. The cells have been enlarged to create dormitories. Sleep well!

Station 6 was the former residence of the governor of the jail, known as the Governor's Mansion. This is the eeriest place of all. Carol's story gets darker now. A strange spirit, referred to as "the vampire" haunts the back stairwell of this section. For years, prisoners referred to this spirit as a creature who "tries to push your soul out of your body". Carol said, "My grandfather had heard about this vampire. They say it feeds on the sick. No one knows for sure whether this creature's territory extends throughout the jail or not."

Carol recounts the experience of two young men who stayed in the Governor's Mansion in 1994. "One night one of the men retired early for the night. He awoke suddenly to see a shadow standing in the doorway. He turned the light on, but the bulb shattered. The shadow quickly skirted across the room and disappeared in the corner where a set of lockers stood. Workers later discovered a secret passage right where the shadow had vanished."

Does the "vampire" travel the building through the many secret passageways?

An ominous inscription was discovered on the stairwell during renovations of the building in 1972. It reads, "I am a non-veridical Vampire who will vanquish you all. One by one I will ornate your odorous flesh with famished fangs. But Who? Are there 94 or 95 steps to the 9th floor? A book on the top shelf will lead you on the right path."

This quote is accompanied by a circle with inverted letters. Carol explained that it was decided to preserve the inscription but added, "No one is sure what all this means. We do know that a bookshelf did exist at one time on the ninth floor in the matrons' quarters. The inscription has been here for many years.

"At one time a Warden moved into the Governor's Mansion with his family. His eight-year-old son often played in the stairwell. By the time the warden left the prison with his family the son was eleven. The child's personality had drastically changed and he was terrified of the dark."

The stairwell is a very strange place to explore. There is a sensation of being watched and there is a heaviness in the atmosphere. Reading the inscription makes the hair on your neck stand up.

No one could be prepared for the visitation of a spirit in the sixth floor stairwell. Here in the stairwell is an arched alcove with a ledge where security guards could chain a prisoner who was giving them difficulty. It is a space now bricked up except for a hole between two bricks.

Five years ago the authorities invited a group of psychics to investigate the hauntings. They claimed that 13 active spirits existed in the building and another 150 souls returned there on the anniversary of their deaths. This is a phenomenal amount of activity for one building and particularly for a hostel.

Carol adds, "One psychic felt very drawn to this wall (the sixth floor alcove). She felt the spirit of a dead prisoner was still here. She suggested that I try putting my hand in the hole between the bricks, something she herself had done. I did it. Not for long, though. It was a moment I'll never forget. My hand felt like ice!

"After the psychics left, things went crazy. Doors would lock and we could hear voices throughout the building. In the evening after the front offices were closed the computers would turn on by themselves and begin to print out incoherent pages of text. The phones kept ringing, but no one was there. This went on for three days."

On the ninth floor we entered what was once the hospital and later became the female inmate cell area. It is now the home of two lounges for the hostel. The carpeted area in the lounge was once the doctor's office and the wooden-floor area was once the operating room, a disturbing thought.

Carol added, "The hospital area was only used from 1862 to 1867. In those days prisoners, if they were lucky, were allowed to shower once a month. Infection was a major health problem in the jail. Inmates would often lose a limb as a result of unsanitary conditions. They were given a shot of whiskey to numb the pain while a doctor removed one of their limbs with a saw!" According to Carol, no records were kept, the hospital was too expensive to maintain and it was subsequently closed.

Officials then renovated the area for female and children prisoners. Young boys were jailed here until age 12 when they were placed in a regular cell block in the jail. The women and children were allowed one bath per week and were required to share the bathwater.

Children's voices are often heard on this floor, especially in the lounge where a crib is located today. Wade Kirkpatrick said, "We would often hear noises in the lounge. When we went to investigate all we found were guests watching the television with the volume low. Obviously, they hadn't heard anything. Periodically we could hear women screaming here."

Ottawa International Hostel

ABOVE: Former inmates hanged at the jail still remain, haunting death row. One evil spirit is reported to inhabit the corner of the hallway. Lights often flicker and cell doors slam shut in this area.

RIGHT: Prisoners had no space to move. Their cells had no plumbing nor electricity.

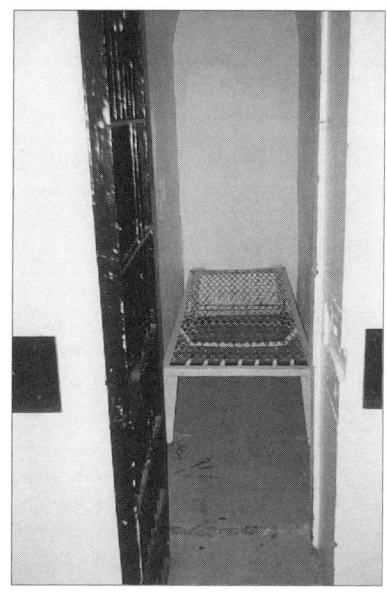

Guests and visitors of the jail can tour the gallows. The hangman's noose still swings from the rafter inside.

Unmarked graves are said to occupy the courtyard area. It was here where jail guards burned the bodies of Irish immigrants.

Ottawa International Hostel

Something remains hidden behind this wall. A frigid draft can be felt escaping from the dislodged bricks.

This eerie stairwell leads to the quarantine area where immigrants awaited their fate. Many souls welcomed death.

In February of 1899 a male prisoner escaped to the women's cell area on the ninth floor. From there he fled to the bathroom in the hallway. There were no bars on the bathroom windows at that time. He fell to his death. A second man made the same attempt. Both legs were broken in the fall and he crawled across the street to the City Registry Office. Carol adds, "The guards rushed out across the street and shot him dead." A third prisoner successfully escaped through the same window but was apprehended and shot to death on a street in Ottawa.

Station 8, the original male cellblock, was once called the "Drum". The cells measure one metre by three metres, (3 feet by 9 feet). There are twenty cells located here. Prisoners were locked inside these cells for 12 hours at night. They spent the other 12 hours of the day locked outside their cells. The hostel has no plans to renovate this area into dorms, so that visitors can still see and feel what a cellblock was like. A few people have attempted to sleep in a cell, but have reported an uncomfortable sleep and a deep feeling of uneasiness. This is quite understandable since the gallows are nearby and death row is just on the other side of the cellblock. Clanging cell bars and voices are heard in this area.

Station 9 is death row. Unexplained phenomena and bizarre accidents have occurred in this part of the jail. Death row consisted of four cells, numbered one to four.

Patrick Whelan spent ten months in cell four awaiting his execution. He was convicted in 1869, on circumstantial evidence, of killing Thomas D'Arcy McGee, one of the Fathers of Confederation. Whelan and 18 others were arrested for the crime. The other 18 were acquitted for lack of evidence,

Ottawa International Hostel

but Whelan was hanged for the murder.

During his ten months on death row, Patrick and his personal guard, John Lyle, became close friends. Mr. Lyle believed Whelan was innocent but could do nothing to stop the hanging. Whelan and Lyle still stalk the halls of death row. They have been heard and seen.

There were three official hangings in the gallows here at the Carleton County Goal. Canada's last public hanging was of Patrick Whelan in 1869. There were 5,000 curious onlookers.

Many superstitious traditions surrounded hangings. People were hanged on the 13th day of the month. If that was not possible, then the hanging would take place on the 13th hour of the day. The hangman always stood on the left side of the prisoner because the right was said to be the divine side. The hangman always tied the noose 13 times. Patrick Whelan was hanged at 11:00 a.m., February 11, 1869.

People staying in the hostel have reported seeing Patrick Whelan sitting in his cell writing at a desk. He may still be writing the letter he wrote to Sir John A. MacDonald to profess his innocence.

Some people believe Patrick Whelan haunts death row because he was hung on the 11th hour, on the 11th day. Other reasons may be his innocence of the crime and the broken promise to send his body to his wife in Montreal.

His gravesite in the courtyard was discovered a few years ago when the City of Ottawa built the Mackenzie King Bridge and expropriated part of the courtyard that had, at one time, extended a considerable distance from the building. Whelan was identified by a ring on his finger. Construction workers discovered 140 gravesites in total. It is a concern for some that more bodies were buried beside the building and in the present-day parking area.

Death row is reported to be haunted by several spirits. Carol said, "Death row is haunted by an evil spirit. No one knows who or what it is. The spirit lives in the corner of the hall. You can feel its presence. The air becomes heavy like before a thunderstorm. The lights flicker or dim. Some visitors see flickering lights along the wall across from the cells. Years ago there were oil lamps on that wall.

"A female visitor attempted several times to open one of the cell doors. The door was sealed. No matter how hard she tried, the door would not open. The cell door had no lock on it. Nothing should have prevented that door from opening.

"The third cell door on death row has been jammed for years. No one can open it. This is the cell where people report hearing three knocks. The psychics agreed that four of the thirteen spirits haunting the jail are here on death row. At one time two iron doors were located on either side of death row. They were removed after an unexplained accident. An employee lost a finger when, without reason or warning, one of the doors slammed shut on his finger. One window on death row shuts all by itself."

A set of showers are located at the end of this hall for the guests who are staying in the hostel. It is common for people who come out of the shower to find their clothes strewn down the hall in front of the death-row cells. Personal possessions have been found in the cells, often a watch that has stopped ticking.

The cell doors clang shut as people pass them. Late one night after conducting a tour, Carol had to return to death row. "This area is so haunted. I was walking down death row, passing the cells, when I came to the cell Patrick Whelan had been in. Even though it was August this one area was many degrees colder. I just kept on walking and didn't look back. In the past we have had a contest for anyone willing to sleep all night on death row. Most people fled before 1:00 a.m."

If you need a room in Ottawa for the night you might consider the Ottawa International Hostel, but be sure to keep your eye on your clothes, your watch and your nerves!

The Ghost of Tom Thomson Canoe Lake

 wandering spirit paddles the dark waters of Canoe Lake in Algonquin Park.

When a woman or man is murdered their soul often remains the prisoner of the circumstance. They remain on in the vicinity of the crime. For nearly a century, the death of Tom Thomson on Canoe Lake in 1917 has remained a mystery. Was it accidental drowning or was it murder? The existence of his spirit on Canoe Lake could support the theory of murder. You be the judge.

Tom Thomson was born in Claremont, Ontario, on August 4, 1877. At the age of two months, his parents, along with his six brothers and sisters, moved to the town of Leigh near Owen Sound on Georgian Bay.

As a young boy he thoroughly enjoyed the outdoors, fishing in the bay, swimming and boating. Tom had an ear for music and played the violin, mandolin and coronet. He was also fascinated by birds and the colour of leaves in the autumn and flowers in the spring. According to his brother, George, he paid keen attention to the seasonal movements of animals. As a teenager he was strongly-built and stood almost two metres (six feet). Judge Little, author of THE TOM THOMSON MYSTERY, adds, "Conversely he couldn't find satisfaction in study; he neither finished high school nor completed a machinists' apprenticeship started in his late teens at Owen Sound. He also attempted, but never completed, a business course at Chatham."

It was in 1901, at the age of 24, that Tom took his first step toward a career in art. He followed his brothers, George and Henry, to Seattle and there joined a commercial art studio where George had begun a year earlier. There Tom explored the territory of his imagination; there he began experimenting with crayon and then water colour sketches. Some mention has been given to an unsuccessful romance with a woman in Seattle, which fostered his return to Toronto in 1905. There he found employment with a commercial art firm.

In 1911 he acquired a new job with the firm of Grip Limited. It was here that he made contact with other kindred spirits—J.E.H. MacDonald, Arthur Lismer, Fred Varley, Tom MacLean, A.Y. Jackson and Frank Carmichael. Now 34 years old, Tom had begun to do sketches and oil paintings around Toronto near the Don Valley, Rosedale Ravine, Scarlet Road, Old Mill and Lambton.

In early 1912 Tom made his first trek to picturesque Canoe Lake in Algonquin Park. Between 1913 and 1917 he painted there from spring break-up until late fall. The majority of his works were inspired here, including 'Northern River', 'West Wind', 'Spring Ice', 'Jack Pine' and 'Northern Lights'. He painted 24 major canvasses and made more than 300 sketches.

Judge William T. Little quoted park ranger Mark Robinson, who first met Thomson in the spring of 1912, in his book, "One evening as I went to Canoe Lake, a couple of other rangers had joined me. It was quite routine in those days for park rangers to inspect all newcomers coming into the park because poaching was a major offense and a common occurrence in the park. As the train came in and drew to a stop, a tall fine-looking man with a packsack on his back stepped off the train. The stranger inquired where he could find a place to stay, and where he could get a good bed and good eats. I explained to him that the Algonquin Hotel was a short distance away and Mowat Lodge was nearby. A man by the name of Fraser served good meals there and had excellent beds. Tom said that was the place for him."

Mowat Lodge became his home away from home. In the ensuing years Tom lived with the Frasers as if one of the family. He even designed a cover for the Frasers' booklet to announce Mowat Lodge. Tom was, nevertheless, a loner and often canoed out into the lake to disappear for days on end, painting and fishing to his heart's content. He was an amiable man with rugged, lean, muscular good looks. Tom was well-liked by most who met him and enjoyed the company of others at the many parties in the area.

Mark Robinson points out that Tom earned his way in the park by purchasing a guide license, and subsequently lead parties of fishermen through the park. He often tented on the east side of Canoe Lake, opposite Mowat Landing, just north of Hayhurst's Point.

In April of 1917 Tom arrived at Canoe Lake for the last

time. On July 7 of that year Tom and a number of local cottage residents met at George Rowe's cabin for some merriment. Drinking at these social events usually lead to storytelling. The topic of the war arose and Tom spoke of his determination to join up as a fire ranger. His earlier attempts to join had been thwarted because of his flat feet. That night a man who we will call "Harvey Button" who was considered to have a bad temperament, only exacerbated by heavy drinking, arrived at the party.

Judge Little wrote, "One young American cottager in particular (Harvey Button) who was of German background, was most outspoken regarding the progress of the war and his forecast of ultimate German supremacy. During the early summer Tom and Martin seemed to share a mutual dislike. These two men, during this Saturday evening, were actually prevented from coming to blows only by the good-natured efforts of the guides. On leaving the cabin before midnight, Button hurled a final threat, 'Don't get in my way if you know what's good for you'."

A love triangle can be a source of great pain and jealousy. Secret love is even more entangling and complex. Winnie Trainor was, by all accounts, a beautiful, mysterious woman. Hidden to most, Winnie and Tom shared a secret love. Judge Little said, "Not until Miss Trainor's death in 1962 has it been known authoritatively that Thomson intended to marry her. Did Harvey Button resent Tom's visits to Winnie Trainor, just next door to him, during those long summer evenings? Did Tom resent Harvey's presence so close to Miss Trainor's cottage?"

Terence Trainor McCormick, the nephew and beneficiary of Miss Trainor's estate, once stated about the letters written between Winnie and Tom, "...the correspondence gave undisputable evidence that Tom and my Aunt were engaged to be married." Their covenant remains a secret known only to them.

It was a rather dull morning and wet on Sunday, July 8, 1917. Shannon Fraser and Tom threw a line in the water at the dam between Joe and Canoe Lakes. Mark Robinson caught sight of the men returning. Tom waved to Mark and called, "Howdy, Mark." Mark acknowledged the greeting. It would be the last time he ever saw Tom alive.

Tom returned to his quarters where he gathered up his tackle box and a loaf of bread and some bacon from Mowat Lodge. He bid farewell to Shannon as his canoe cut a path across the waters of Canoe Lake. Shannon watched his friend head down the west side of the lake. The time was 12:50 p.m. Guests staying at Mowat Lodge watched Tom disappear past Little Wapomeo Island only one and a half kilometres (one mile) away.

The following day Harvey Button casually remarked to some guests at Mowat Lodge that he had spotted an upturned canoe between Little and Big Wapomeo Islands. Apparently, he and his sister had not stopped, but continued on for an afternoon fishing excursion. On their return trip the canoe had disappeared.

No one seemed too concerned about such a report. It was a strange reaction by such a small community of residents who all knew the boats on the lake. Judge Little adds, "Furthermore, Canoe Lake residents considered it strange that Harvey Button could not have recognized Thomson's grey-green canoe with a metal strip on the keel side; it was known to everyone on Canoe Lake at the time."

Charlie Scrim found the craft the following morning behind Big Wapomeo Island. Mark Robinson said, "Contrary to some people who may tell you the canoe was floating right side up, there was none of his equipment in the canoe, except his portaging paddle, which was lashed in position for carrying, and the ground sheet with bread and bacon in the bow section. There were no fishing poles, no gear; even his small axe was gone."

Robinson immediately reported to Park Superintendent Bartlett who authorized a search. Tom's brother, George, was contacted. He arrived at Canoe Lake on July 12th. Dynamite was exploded in the lake without the desired results—no body surfaced.

The sharp eyes and minds of guides George Rowe and Charlie Scrim noted that Tom's own working paddle was missing. Especially strange was how the portaging paddle was lashed in a position to portage. It had been knotted in a most unorthodox way. Only an inexperienced canoeist would fashion such a knot. Thomson was an expert canoeist and outdoorsman.

On July 14 George Thomson gathered up a number of Tom's sketches and caught the train back to New York. He felt there was little he could do.

On the morning of July 15, 1917, Dr. G.W. Howland spotted something lying low in the water by Hayhurst Point on the east shore of Canoe Lake. At first he thought it was a loon. At the same time George Rowe and Lowrie Dickson were paddling down the middle of the lake when they saw the doctor hailing them. The canoeists aimed for the object. It was Tom. He was dead.

They towed the body to a campsite on Big Wapomeo, approximately 300 metres (100 yards) ahead. There at Big Wap, a campout halfway down the west side of the lake, they tied the body to tree roots in a shallow. The guides then notified Dr. Howland and Mark Robinson who contacted Superintendent Bartlett.

Dr. A.E. Ranney, a coroner living in North Bay, was notified. He did not arrive on the train the next day. Robinson was frantic and informed his Superintendent that something needed to be done with the body. It was not right to leave it in the blazing sun. The Superintendent informed Mark to have Dr. Howland examine the body. Dr. Howland was a Toronto medical doctor and a professor of neurology at the University of Toronto who was vacationing on Wapomeo Island. Mark then ordered a casket and rough box for the burial.

On the morning of July 17th Dr. Howland examined the deceased. Mark helped to remove a length of fishing line that was wrapped 16 or 17 times around Tom's left ankle. That was odd. There was no water in the lungs. Across the left temple was a mark that looked as though he had been struck with the edge of a paddle. The doctor's report read: "A bruise on left temple the size of 4 inches long, no other sign of external marks visible on body, air issuing from mouth, some bleeding from right ear. Cause of death, drowning."

Tom was placed in a casket and moved to the mainland for a hurried funeral. A small congregation of Canoe Lake residents and guides, including Miss Trainor, witnessed the burial at Canoe Lake Cemetery. Miss Trainor caught the evening train for Huntsville. She would never again greet her lover by the water's edge. Or would she?

A short time later a telegram arrived to the attention of Shannon Fraser. It was a request by Mr. H.W. Churchill, a Huntsville undertaker, to exhume the body. Apparently the family had requested that Tom be interred near the family home at Leith, Ontario. At 8:00 p.m. Fraser met the eastbound train at Canoe Lake Station. Churchill got off the train wearing a dark suit and bowler hat. He informed Fraser that he had a metal casket with him and asked that Fraser give him a hand to put it on his wagon.

With a call to the horses they were off. Fraser was stunned to learn that Churchill was going to remove the body that very night. It all seemed very strange. Fraser remarked that he couldn't get any help until the next day.

Judge Little quoted the following conversation, "The undertaker replied, 'I don't need any help, just get me a good digging shovel, a lantern and a crow bar and I'll do the rest.'

"'Here we are,' announced Shannon. 'Do you still want to do this job tonight without any help?'

"'Just pick me up about midnight and I'll be ready,' replied the undertaker."

Fraser returned at midnight to give Churchill a hand to place the casket on the rear baggage floor of the coach and transport the body to the train station. Judge Little highlights an oddity that occurred, "Fraser was to comment a number of times later, 'It just didn't impress me the weight was distributed the way it should be with a body in it.'"

Judge Little also documented Mark Robinson's comments, " 'The Superintendent called me up and said, "Go down to the cemetery and if they haven't filled the grave in, fill it in." I went down. Now, in one corner of the grave was a hole I wouldn't say it would be more than 20 inches and about a depth (Mark indicated about 18 inches by his hand), God forgive me if I'm wrong, but I still think Thomson's body is over there (Mark pointed to the hillside gravesite where Tom was originally interred).' "

In the 1950s Judge Little and three other men, Jack Eastaugh, Leonard Gibson and Frank Braught decided to investigate the Thomson mystery themselves. They firmly believed Tom was still buried in the Canoe Lake Cemetery. The Judge was convinced he had been murdered. Armed with shovels and axes the men began to clear the underbrush. At two metres (six feet) they found nothing. Another attempt at a different spot revealed nothing. Then Jack called out from beside a spruce tree. There were depressions a metre (3 feet) wide in the ground. They began to dig. They struck pay dirt. The shovel found the remains of a rough pine box. No name was inscribed on the box. There was no evidence of metal remnants, such as buttons, belt buckle, shoe nails nor clothing.

Judge Little described the scene, "We saw parts of the casket lining and what appeared to be possibly a cotton or light canvas shroud. We recalled that, after Tom's examination by Dr. Howland, the body was immediately placed in a casket wrapped only in a shroud due to the removal of clothes related to the advanced state of decomposition of the body. We also discovered a hole in the skull region of the temple which coincided with the region indicated at both the inquest and in Mark Robinson's observations of a blow to the temple."

A short time later Dr. Harry Ebbs and Dr. Noble Sharpe of the Ontario Provincial Criminal Laboratory arrived at Canoe Lake. They gathered the skeletal remains and photographed the skull with its puncture at the temple.

Dr. Sharpe later concluded, "The bones were definitely male. Calculations from humerus, femur and tibia gave an estimated height of 5'8". These bones suggested also a robust, well-muscled person."

Professor J.C.B Grant, of the Department of Anthropology, University of Toronto, was asked for his opinion. He stated, "The skeleton was of a male, strong, height 5'8" plus or minus 2", age in late 20s and of Mongolian type, either Indian or nearly full-breed Indian."

Further studies were made of the skull, including x-rays. According to Judge Little, "X-ray of the skull before emptying out the sand showed no bullet in the skull and none found in the sand after emptying. The hole in the left temple region is nearly three-quarters of an inch (less than 2 cm) in diameter. The inner plate opening is slightly wider showing a slight bevelling. No radiating fractures were seen in x-ray. There was no injury on the inner table of the skull opposite the hole where a bullet would impinge. The orbital plate and nasal bones were so intact that no bullet could have escaped from the skull." Therefore, the hole in the temple was not the result of a bullet wound.

Professor Eric Linnel of the Department of Neuropathology concluded, "The wound, however, though definitely not due to a bullet, could be caused by a sharp instrument such as a pick, a narrow hammer head." Maybe a paddle?

Judge Little responded to the investigation, "The foot of the grave in which the bones were found was 21' (seven metres) due north of the corner of the fence surrounding the two marked graves. This is certainly approximately where Mr. Thomson was buried originally. There is nothing to prove that the opened grave is not the same as Mr. Thomson's and the coffin is just as his was said to be."

Why so much conflicting information? Did this group of men really dig up the remains of Tom Thomson? There should have been no body at all!

Jane Loftus, the daughter of the late Judge Little, states, "My father always believed the body they found in Canoe Lake Cemetery was that of Tom Thomson."

In 1935 Miss Blodwen Davies, an official of the Saskatchewan Art Board, published a biography of Tom Thomson. It was while doing the research for the book that she investigated his death. She concluded, "I came away from my investigation with the conviction there had been foul play. I tried to get the Ontario Government to open an investigation but they said it had all happened so long ago it was best to leave it alone."

Miss Davies spent the rest of her life pursuing the mystery. She once wrote concerning the testimony at the inquest, "No one remarked that only a living body could be bruised or bleed, or that Thomson's lungs were filled with air, not with water."

A questionnaire she used with Mark Robinson is reprinted courtesy of the Archives of Canada, Ottawa:

QUESTION: How deep was the water in which Thomson was found?
ANSWER: About 30 feet (10 metres).
QUESTION: How far was it from shore?
ANSWER: 125 yards (120 metres).
QUESTION: Was his fishing rod and line found?
ANSWER: No.
QUESTION: Do you think it was his own line which was wound around his ankle?
ANSWER: It might have been his own line but not his regular fishing line.
QUESTION: Did you see a mark on his forehead and if so, what was it like?
ANSWER: A slight bruise over the eyebrow.
QUESTION: Did the Buttons aid in the search for Thomson?
ANSWER: They did on the Lake. They did not search in the woods as far as I know.
QUESTION: Did they make any attempt to direct the search?
ANSWER: No. They were very quiet in every way.

So many of Thomson's friends were puzzled over his death. Many did not believe that he had drowned. Miss Davies adds, "Why did Thomson's body take eight days to rise in a shallow lake in the middle of July? Bodies that have been in warm summer waters usually rise after a couple of days, due to bloating. Could the fishing line bound round the lower left leg have been tied to some weighty object such as a stone?

"If Tom struck his head on rocks after death, how could the body bleed? Bodies do not bruise or bleed after death.

This man was not accident prone; he was a canoeist of exceptional skill. The weather and water conditions were calm. It is difficult to believe he just fell out of his canoe and received a severe wound to his head."

Tom Thomson has never left Canoe Lake. Speculation says that he was murdered and he was in love. Just ask Mrs. Northway and Canadian artist, Lawren Harris, who resided in the park in the summer of 1931. They believe he appeared on the waters that year.

Judge Little recorded their experience, "It had been a happy day and ever so lazy. At dusk we were coming home, tired, rested, and at peace with the world. It was a tremendously still evening, you could hear the silence against your ear. The hills made strange, statuesque figures against the haunting orange of the western sky, while the first star set its light akindle, as an alter lamp of the universe against the canopy of the after glow. Even my guide's tales had ceased, and through my mind drifted fragments of harmonies as if heard from a far away 'cello'. Suddenly the voice of my guide shattered the silence. 'They're coming out to meet us from the portage.'

"And turning toward the sunset I saw a man kneeling in a canoe that slowly came towards us. 'So they are', I answered. 'I guess we are pretty late'.

"My guide turned from his course in order that we might better meet our herald, now a little less than a hundred yards (90 metres) away. I raised my voice and called, and waved my hand, while my guide kept paddling toward the camper. But there was no response, for even as we looked the canoe and its paddler, without warning or sound, vanished into nothingness, and on the undisturbed lake were only our lonely selves and the shrieking of a loon."

Miss Northway added some observations her mother had left out of the story, "As my mother was coming into the bay by the portage, she saw a canoe and a paddler in a yellow shirt. 'They're coming out from the portage to meet us', said the guide. The man waved and the guide waved back. Then the paddler, canoe and all, completely vanished.

"My father and Mr. Taylor Statten, being practical people, on hearing the tale, insisted it had been a mirage, but Lawren Harris was sure it was the spirit of Tom Thomson. His rationale was that those who depart before their time continue to haunt the lands they loved.

"My mother was inclined to accept Lawren's interpretation, much to my father's disgust. A point that was much discussed, but never settled, was what colour of shirt was Tom wearing when he was drowned?"

For years people have reported seeing a phantom canoeist travelling the waters of Algonquin Park. One moment you see a man paddling a canoe across the way and in the next, he vanishes. Many eye-witness accounts refer to the canoeist as Tom Thomson. One witness to such an event was drawn to paint the experience.

Doug Dunford is a professional artist best known for his ability to capture the symbols of Muskoka life in high realist style. He lives in the Muskokas.

Early in his career he was given one of A.Y. Jackson's easels and one of his old chairs. These were his first connections to the Group of Seven painters, but others followed.

Fishing was a passion of Tom Thomson's. No one could explain why a length of fishing line was wrapped 16 or 17 times around his left ankle at the time of his death.

ABOVE: The Trainor cottage remains a historic landmark of Canoe Lake. Family still use the cabin during the summer.

LEFT: Few pictures exist of Winnie Trainor. Even her home in Huntsville was torn down shortly after her death. Winnie is seen here on the left.

Judge Little had to see for himself if Tom Thomson was still buried at Canoe Lake. From left to right: Leonard Gibson, Little, W. J. Eastaugh and Frank Braught starting to dig. To their amazement they found a body in Thomson's grave.

RIGHT: The skull removed from Thomson's grave indicates a hole at the temple coinciding with the injury sustained by the artist.

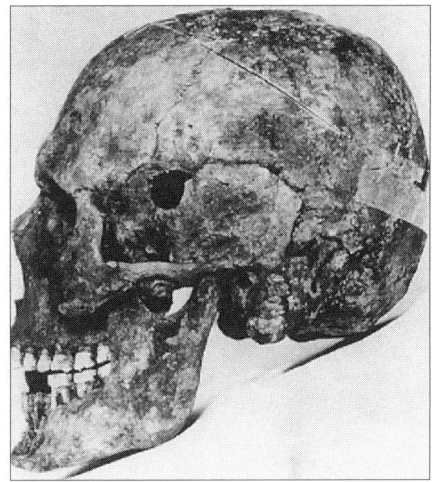

The small graveyard overshadowed by an ancient birch stands on a hilltop beyond Canoe Lake. No signs or path mark the way to this cemetery. It remains hidden in the forest.

The cross marks the original gravesite of Tom Thomson. It was here that Judge Little and his friends found a body in a grave alleged to be empty.

Ghost Of Tom Thomson

In the summer of 1980, Doug found himself painting a new sign for Algonquin Park. For two weeks he immersed himself in the natural beauty of the park. Doug has always believed, "You have to live the art in the environment where you work."

One evening a social gathering took place at a cottage on Canoe Lake. Doug recalls, "The next morning I decided to go down to the dock. A thick mist was enshrouding Canoe Lake. I just stood on the dock with my camera hanging around my neck, looking. Then I heard this trickling sound like a paddle in the water. Suddenly a person in a canoe emerged from the mist. We made eye contact and then he turned and vanished. For some unknown reason I took his picture just before he turned and disappeared, as abruptly and mystically as he had appeared.

"In that moment I sensed a strange energy. It took me off guard. I have felt that strange energy before. I don't know why I took the picture and began to second-guess the experience. Had it really happened? Would there be anything on the photograph? I didn't understand why this person had turned so abruptly. Why was someone out on the lake in such fog? Why had he disappeared? I got this strange feeling. Maybe in my own consciousness I made a connection. I do know that I can only connect from my own experience. I knew it was Tom Thomson. I was shocked when the film was developed. There was my phantom canoeist.

"I was drawn to paint the photograph. A good painting depicts what you have experienced. This photograph was a memory of the moment. The painting chooses you. It is always there. It never leaves. One day something triggers it.

Within six months after the experience, I painted it. Then I painted over it. I wasn't ready. It didn't feel right.

"When I told people the story they agreed that it indeed could be Tom Thomson. Six or seven years later I did a small watercolour of that dramatic experience on Canoe Lake.

"Then one day, during a show in my gallery, a young man walked in. He was going to school out west. This piece of work, entitled 'The Return of Tom Thomson', was hanging in the show. The man purchased it. About a year later he wrote to me to say that he bought the painting because he had seen the same man in the same canoe in the park. He had felt it had been a ghost himself. He was amazed to see it hanging in my gallery."

On the anniversary of Tom Thomson's death a few people gather on the shore of Canoe Lake to see if he will appear. There is no question, for those who have seen him, that it is Tom.

As for Winnie Trainor, she never married and lived in Huntsville until her death. Jane Loftus pointed out that Miss Trainor would often travel to Canoe Lake and place flowers on the grave of Tom Thomson. Perhaps she never married because she knew he was still there with her. If she saw him and communicated with him, she kept it to herself.

Playwright Stina Nyquist in her Tom Thomson play, 'The Shantyman's Daughter', has Miss Trainor say this about herself, "I'm a slob. I've been one since that summer a long time ago. I let my hair go. I have soup stains on my blouse, my stockings are rumpled, and so on and so forth. It's not that I'm a slob at heart. I'm not a natural-born slob. I just got that way, bit by bit, since that summer. But once every year, on this day, I dress up. I go to the beauty parlor, I put on this outfit, and this hat—if it's not too windy. I got this dress for a special occasion that didn't happen...."

There are many unexplained events on Canoe Lake. One young girl, Sarah, found a painting tucked in a crack in a tree and an old piece of wood inscribed with a biblical quote. Does she have a Tom Thomson original? Who is creating mystical art in Algonquin Park?

There are power boats on the lake now. There are mysteries and there are many unanswered questions for curious visitors.

The Orchards, Prince Albert

In HAUNTED ONTARIO I alluded to the haunting of my previous home. This is the full story:

"The Orchards" was a beautiful home built in Prince Albert, Ontario by James McBrien in 1870 for his bride. He was the first inspector of public schools for the Province of Ontario under Edgar Ryerson. His home was built in the Cape-Cod tradition of white clapboard with green shutters and trim. It had a magnificent cabriole veranda and a two-storey summer kitchen with servants' quarters upstairs.

The McBrien family was a well-educated, artistic, musical and spiritually- active family. There was one 'black sheep', a troublesome son named Sydney who did things like sell the family chickens for money to buy himself a drink or two.

All in all they were an upstanding family, well-respected in the community; folks smiled when Major General James H. McBrien Junior rode his horse to town to get the mail. James McBrien Junior spent some years in the North West Mounted Police and saw service in the South African War. From there he went to Australia on military service and the

Military College at Camberley, England, where he studied military technique. During the First World War he was appointed to the General taff. He was later Chief of Staff at Ottawa, becoming the head of affairs in the Department of Militia and Defence. He retired as the head of the Royal Canadian Mounted Police. His sister, Julia McBrien, was a concert pianist who travelled to Persia and California. Another sister, Elizabeth, produced art that can be seen in the National Art Gallery. The Orchards remained in the family for a hundred years. It was bought in 1970 by Joe and Dolores Victor who sought a place for Guirdjieffan groupwork intensives. The Victors shared a toast and sealed a deal with the two remaining elderly McBrien sisters who still occupied the house. The spiritual history was to continue.

When the Victors moved in, they discovered that the home had been left completely as they had first seen it. No furniture had been removed; even the clothes were hanging in the closet. The pictures on the walls and the sherry glasses the McBrien sisters had used were still on the coffee table. It was incredible.

There was a hundred years of family history to be seen around them—a penny farthing bicycle, a beautiful harp, decades of period furniture and valuables, a three-holer outhouse in the back and an elaborate old cookstove in the summer kitchen. Dolores made herself right at home and it wasn't too long before she discovered they were not 'alone'. The two elderly sisters had moved to a nursing home but 'someone' was there.

Among the things that happened was the constant slamming of the hall door that adjoined the house to the sum-

The Orchards

mer kitchen. It would slam in her face; it would slam in her back. Her bed would shake as if to fall apart. She was a strong woman, a spiritualist and not easily intimidated—ever! She told her unseen housemates "This is my house now. You live here if you like but leave me alone. Stop slamming doors and shaking beds. I've had enough!" Surprisingly enough, that mischievous, poltergeist activity abated. Although Dolores proceeded to bring down the summer kitchen and add a weaving studio she left the main house to remain as it was. She would say, "The studio is mine; the main house is 'their' period".

One day, however, Susy came to live there. Susy was Dolores' mother and she was 'getting on'. She had some trouble getting around and was prone, when she did, to being a problem. Susy smoked. Well, our spirits didn't like that, or did they? Did our spirit want the cigarettes gone? Or did our spirit want the cigarettes? Sidney had been the rebel after all! Susy could never keep a pack long enough to smoke it. The cigarettes would simply disappear and would usually turn up in another room.

In 1976 I met Dolores Victor. I was a journalist/entrepreneur with my own magazine and I had gone to interview her for a feature article. I discovered her to be an intriguing, delightful and somewhat awe-inspiring woman. Together we, along with some others, gave birth that year to a school for artistic and cultural pursuits which we called "The School of Creativity". We taught Tai Chi, poetry, watercolours, drama and calligraphy. Over the years it was incorporated as the J. McBrien School of Creativity. Spiritual Courses, Healing Techniques and Native Studies started in 1983 and the name changed to "Heartland".

Dolores often spoke about the early seventies when she was redecorating. It was a frustrating period. The painters quit because the lid kept being put on the paint can and their tools would go missing unless she stayed right there with them. The man repairing the stairs constantly had his hammer taken downstairs or upstairs when he wanted it left on the stairs. A man was frequently seen rocking on the verandah. A woman, in a long gown, 'lived' in the blue room at the top of the stairs and it remained undecorated and unrepaired until 1980. She was also seen walking in the back yard. She resembled the photographs of Julia McBrien.

I had occasion to stay over one evening. It was my first encounter with the active spirit world there. (Little did I realize that it would be here that I would meet my life partner, Allana, here that I would come to live, here that I would begin my career as a writer and here that I would find material to put in my book about HAUNTED ONTARIO.)

That first night, however, I was horrified. This stately, old home certainly could have been the subject of a ghost movie. It was and still is the most awe-inspiring and architecturally-divine structure to ever have been built in the village of Prince Albert. It is reminiscent of a southern plantation estate.

That particular night Dolores had directed me to the upstairs bedroom on the right hand side of the hall in the front of the house. There, I was to spend the night. No one else was living on the second floor at the time. I remember slipping under the covers and drifting off to sleep. It seemed so peaceful. In the night I had what I thought was a vivid dream. I saw a group of people walking down the second floor hallway carrying a coffin. One member of the party was dragging his leg. It spooked me. The next morning I related it to Dolores. She nodded knowingly. I questioned her. She told me that my dream was not a dream. She said that what I had dreamed had actually taken place in another time there.

What I had witnessed was the funeral of James McBrien. The gentlemen who was dragging his leg was his brother, Sydney. Sydney had injured his leg in an accident many years before.

Allana lived with Dolores Victor from 1979 to 1993, first with her husband, John and her children, Jeremy and Sarah, and after 1986, with me. She has a long account of 'unexplained activity'.

"I first moved to 350 Simcoe St. in 1979. I had experienced paranormal activity there prior to that when I had helped to run an antique store there from August 1977 to 1979. Cigarettes would always go missing. One day in 1978, I visited my mentor-friend, Dolores, because I was in a very saddened state. She had an appointment in the city. She said I was welcome to stay there as long as I wished. At that time she lived there alone. Five of us, in those days, gathered there in an alcove of the studio each morning for meditation and once a week for spiritual readings. I chose to stay there in the alcove to console myself. The tears flowed, but eventually it seemed more sensible to pray for help and I did. Almost immediately there was a 'presence' that filled the space, a presence of peace and love and comfort unlike anything I had ever encountered. I sat there for some undetermined length of time before I went on about my day and, in fact, my life.

"In 1979 it seemed that whenever I was alone in the house I would be 'followed' by a heavy, persistent energy that almost felt menacing. The following year 'something' sat on me one night in bed and made it very difficult to breathe. Dolores suggested I send the presence packing by repeating the Lord's Prayer and telling it to go. It took three repetitions but whatever it was, it did leave.

"Objects on the refrigerator in the studio kitchen flew off on a regular basis and came close to hurting people many times. At one time that had been the location of a set of stairs to the second floor of the summer kitchen. Maybe 'spirits' walk there still.

"In 1984 and 1986 I 'saw' James McBrien, Junior standing in full-dress R.C.M.P. uniform on the landing above the studio. Other people have also seen him there. At that time I had not seen any photos of him but when we bought the home in 1989 we found many old McBrien photo albums. I was astounded to find that he was exactly as I had seen him.

"Dolores passed over in March, 1989.

"Four of us bought the house and rented out rooms to meet the high monthly overhead. One evening tempers flared and the tension was high. We all retired at about 10:00 o'clock. I was awakened by a loud, hollow, humming drone, sort of musical in tone, at 11:00 p.m. It could have been a sound in the pipes and I set out to investigate. To my surprise the sound existed in our bedroom, the laundry room below and the bathroom above, but could not be heard anywhere else in the house. Odd. I awakened someone else in the house, Iris, and together we proceeded to 'sit in the sound'. The sound was in a vertical column that penetrated the house, approximately one meter in diameter (four feet). Within the column you could not hear yourself think, it was so loud; outside the column it was still a loud, audible sound; in the hall outside the room it was not possible to hear it at all. We could not understand the phenomenon but felt that it was not threatening. We sat in it until it stopped. It lasted one hour exactly. To my knowledge it has never happened again. I have since read that this is a phenomenon that can occur where two lay-lines intersect. Lay-lines are magnetic lines that exist within the body of the earth and conduct current for the planet. Where they cross there are power points and phenomena occur such as power surges, trees growing in spirals and other unusual growth patterns.

"In 1990 a friend and I were talking in the upstairs hall during an electrical storm. I was tired and we sat down for our conversation. We had no more than sat down when a round ball of light, about 30 centimeters (15 inches) in diameter moved in through the window, 'rolled' through the air down the hall and passed through the other end with no visible effect on the house.

"We had a friend do a spirit cleansing of the house in 1991 because it was a worry for some members of the household. We were told that the spirits might go or stay as they were free to decide for themselves. I saw James McBrien at least twice more before we moved in 1993 but most of the other activity seemed to settle down. There was still a problem with articles disappearing and reappearing as well as almost audible conversations and other sounds in the hall.

"Our dogs never did go upstairs unaccompanied and my daughter Sarah preferred to have a pet for company and a lock on her door."

Music can be an expression or ordered movement of the forces of a world with which we rarely come in contact. Some spiritualists believe that all thought expresses itself through sound. People hear this sound as a lovely yet indescribable series of ever-changing chords, akin to the sound of harps or pipes. Angels are considered to be one class of spirit who are devoted to music and habitually express themselves in this way. Old Hindu books under the name of Gandharvas say that the man whose soul is in tune with music will most certainly attract the attention of angels and will draw himself into connection with some of them. Famous composers such as Bach, Beethoven, Mendelssohn, Handel and Mozart could hear this sound. Some of them spoke of hearing the whole of a grand oratorio, a stately march or a noble chorus in one resounding chord.

My first experience of sound from the spirit world came in the mid-1990s when I made a conscious choice to leave southern Ontario and move north to a secluded home in nature. Here I felt that I could be more aware and listen to the sounds of other kingdoms. One morning I awakened to the sound of music. My first thought was that someone had turned the radio on although this was never a common practice. Then I tuned into the sound. Truly, the best way to describe it was 'heavenly'. Although it was faint it seemed to be coming from the second floor of the house. No one lived in that part of our home. The music was like a chorus of instruments and then it vanished. It may have lasted five or ten minutes.

I still hear it periodically, always in the early morning hours; sometimes someone else might hear it. It stopped for a period when we were doing construction but last year it returned. It seems as though the music comes in late evening or early morning. Spiritualists believe this musical manifestation highlights the vivid and glowing life around you.

Allana says, "My personal feelings about our old home are that the McBrien family were attached to this magnificent home and to the high spiritual energy. The crossed lay-lines made interdimensional activity a much greater possibility."

Today that home is a private one, still with an extended family and it is the home yet again 'of spirit'. The new owners have a minister among them.

Acknowledgements

For their stories, advice and help in researching HAUNTED ONTARIO 2, I wish to thank:

Bruce Bishop, Claudette Boyd, John Cameron, Carol Devine, Doug Dunford, Jane Edmonds, Calay Hall, John Hoodless, Ottilie Hubmann, Kathleen A. Hicks, Wade KirkPatrick, Jack & Patricia Legg, Paul Lloyd, Jane Loftus, Ruth McCuaig, Robert Mikel, Ian & Pam Mollett, Stina Nyquist, Glen Oldford, Barbara Patterson, Sandy Spencer, Guerrino & Anna Maria Staropoli, Candace Steele, Barbara Teatero, Scott Thomas, Cathryn Thompson, Mike Thomson, Pat Quigley and Ian Woodburn.

If you would like to visit ~

Alonguin Provincial Park
Whitney, ON
705 633-5572
www.algonquinpark.on.ca

Avon Theatre
99 Downie Street
Stratford, ON
519 271-0055

Cherry Hill House Restaurant
680 Silvercreek
Cooksville, ON
905 275-9300

Legg's Historic General Store (Birr)
23204 Richmond Street North
R.R. 42
London, ON
519 666-0759

Mackechnie House Bed and Breakfast
173 Tremaine Street
Cobourg, ON
905 372-6242

Massasauga Provincial Park
R.R. 2
Parry Sound, ON
705 378-2401

Mylar & Loreta's Restaurant
Highway 24
Singhampton, ON
705 445-1247

The Ojibway Club
Ojibway Island
Pointe au Baril, ON
705 366-5085

Ottawa International Hostel
75 Nicholas Street
Ottawa, ON
613 235-2595

Pleasant Cove Resort
North Shore Road
Pointe au Baril, ON
705 366-2206

University of Toronto
St. George Campus
Toronto, ON
www.utoronto.ca

Bibliography

Addison, Ottelyn, TOM THOMSON, THE ALGONQUIN YEARS, McGraw-Hill Ryerson Ltd., 1995.

Blodwen, Davies, PADDLE AND PALETTE, Ryerson Press,

Colombo, John, Robert, HAUNTED TORONTO, Hounslow Press, 1996.

Fazakas, Ray, THE DONNELLY ALBUM, Firefly Books, 1995.

Leadbeater, C.W. THE OTHER SIDE OF DEATH, Kessinger Publishing Company, Montana, U.S.A., 1928.

Little, William T., THE TOM THOMSON MYSTERY, McGraw-Hill, 1970.

Mika, Helma & Nick, PLACES IN ONTARIO, Mika Publishing, 1983.

McCuaig, Ruth, H., OUR POINTE AU BARIL, Township of the Archipelago, 1989.

Miller, Orolo, LONDON 200, London Chamber of Commerce, 1988.

Miller, Orolo, THIS WAS LONDON, Butternut Press Inc. Wesport, Ontario.

Nicoll, Maurice, PSYCHOLOGICAL COMMENTARIES, Robinson & Watkins, 1974.

Saunders, Audrey, THE ALGONQUIN STORY, The Ontario
     Department of Lands and Forests, 1946.
Spilsbury, John, R., COBOURG, EARLY DAYS AND MODERN
     TIMES, The Cobourg Committee, 1981.

Plays
Nyquist, Stina, *The Shantyman's Daughter*, Huntsville, 1978.

Newspapers
Bennett, Michael, *The Hamilton Spectator*, "The Hauntings
     of Halton", 1987.
The Parry Sound Star, Obituary Section, May 30, 1968.
Huron Expositor, February, 20, 1880.

Index

Algonquin Park .129-130,142,149
Avon Theatre 43-45
Aylesworth, Allen 26
Beard, Robert 21
Bennett, Michael 33,38
Birr 97-98,100
Bishop, Bruce 19
Blackstone Harbour . . .49-50,52
Boulton, D'Arcy 59
Boyd, Claudette 89-91,95
Brandburger, Albert 44
Brant, Joseph 30-41
Bruckland, Bert 15
Burgis, Mrs. 63-64,69
Burlington 29,39
Burlington Bay 30
Calhoun, Joseph 51
Calhoun, John 50
Cameron, John 14,18
Canoe Lake 129-149
Carleton County Gaol
. 113-116,125
Carmichael, Frank 130

Cascanette, Jerome . .49-52,55,57
Cattermole, William 59
Chatham 130
Cherry Hill House Restaurant
. 71-80
Churchill, H.W. 136
Claremont 129
Cobourg 59-63
Cole, Charles F. 11
Coleman, A.B. 31-32
Collingwood 90,107
Columbo, John Robert 75
Conger (Pine) Lake 50
Davies, Miss Blodwen . . .139-140
Davis, Hamilton C. 11-12,14
Dempsey, Christian 17-18
Devine, Carol
. 115-120,124,126-127
Diabolos, Paul 22-26
Dickson, Lowrie 134
Dogherty, Margaret 114
Donnelly, Tom 99
Donnellys 98

Index

Douglas, Allana 155-159
Dunford, Doug 142, 147-148
Emery, Claire 31
Ford, Barbara 31
Fortune, James 61
Fortune, Alice 61-62
Fraser, Shannon 133, 136
Georgian Bay 86
Grant, J.C.B. 138
Hall, Calay 19
Hampton Hotel 105-106
Harris, Lawren 141-142
Hart House 21
Hicks, Kathleen 73, 75
Howland, Dr. G.W. 134-135
Hubmann, Ottilie 91-95
Huntsville 136, 144, 148
Huron Expositor 99
Inspector Christie 114
Jackson, A.Y. 130, 142
Joseph Brant Museum 29-33
Kernaghan, Ed 18
Kerr, W.J. Simcoe 30-31
King George III 30
Kirkpatrick, Wade 115
Land, Ron 74
Langmuir, J.W. (Inspector) . . .114
Legg, Jack 97-103
Legg's General Store 97-103
Leith 136
Linnel, Eric 138
Lismer, Arthur 130
Little, Judge 130-145
Little & Big Wapomeo
  Islands 133-135
Lloyd, Paul 18-19
London 100
Louden, James 22, 24
Lyle, John 125
MacDonald, J.E.H. 130
MacDonald, Sir John A. 125
Mackechnie, Stuart 60
Mackechnie,
  Anna Marie Poore 61
MacLean, Tom 130
Massassauga Provincial
  Park 49-53
McBrien, James .151, 152, 155, 157
McBrien, Julia 152, 154
McCormick,
  Terence Trainor 132-133
McCuaig, Ruth H. 12-14
McGee, Thomas D'Arcy 124
McLoughlin, Mary 114
McPherson, General .97-100, 103
McQuesten, T.B. 32
Miller, Orlo 100
Milnes, Humphrey 25
Ministry of Natural
  Resources 53
Mississauga 71, 72
Mollet, Ian 85-89, 95
Nicoll, Maurice 84
North Bay 135

Northway, Mrs. 141-142
Nyquist, Stina 148
Ojibway Hotel 11-19
Oldford, Glen 21,25,27
Omahen, Rick 17
Osprey Township 106
Ottawa 125,127
Ottawa International Hostel
. . . . 113,115,127
Owen Sound 129-130
Parry Sound 11,49,86,89,93
Pointe au Baril 11,18-19
Port Hope 68
Prince Albert 151
Ranney, Dr. A.E. 135
Reznikoff, Ivan 22-27
Robinson, Mark
. 131,133-135,137-139
Romain, William Stanislas . . 72,80
Rowe, George 132,134
Ryerson, Edgar 151
Scrim, Charlie 134
Sharpe, Dr. Noble 138
Silverthorn, Joseph 72,75
Silverthorn, Jane 72
Simcoe 111
Sing, Josiah R. 106
Singhampton 105-106
Small, Ambrose 45-46
Smith, John 25
Spencer, Sandy 107,108,110
Staropoli, Guerrino 77

Stone, W.L. 30
Stratford 43
Teatero, Barbara 38
Thomas, Scott 53-55,57
Thompson, Cathryn 62-68
Thomson, Tom 129-149
   artwork 106,130,148
Thomson, George . . 129-130,134
Toronto 21,32,72,107,130
Toronto Star 74
Trainor, Winnie
. . . . 132,136,144,148
Trinity College 23
University of Toronto 21
Urquhart, Ann 38
Varley, Fred 130
Victor, Dolores 152-156
Whelan, Patrick 124-127
Woodburn, Ian 62,65,67
Woods Bay 51

Photo credits

p. 15, 16	Collection of Ruth McCuaig
p. 20 (top)	Metropolitan Toronto Reference Library T30932
(bottom)	Metropolitan Toronto Reference Library T13153
p. 23	Metropolitan Toronto Reference Library T13049
p. 34 (top)	Ivan Cleaver postcard collection, Burlington Public Library
(bottom)	Burlington Historical Society
p. 35	Burlington Historical Society
p. 42	Jane Edmonds, Stratford Festival Archives
p. 45	Stratford Festival Archives
p. 48, 51, 56	Massassauga Provincial Park
p. 58	MacKechnie House
p. 70, 74, 75	Collection of Kathleen A. Hicks
p. 128	Doug Dunford
p. 143, 144	Collection of Jane Loftus
p. 145	Collection of Jane Loftus

all other photographs by Terry Boyle

A note from the author:

This book would not have been possible without the help of the many people who so graciously agreed to be interviewed.

If you, or someone close to you, has a similiar story to share, I would be grateful to hear from you.

>Terry Boyle
>Polar Bear Press
>35 Prince Andrew Place
>Toronto, Ontario M3C 2H2